The Hole in My Soul

From Spiritual Bankruptcy
To Spiritual Abundance

△

By: Kelly M. Spencer

copyright © 2023 Red Door Publishing House

and Kelly M. Spencer

All rights reserved.

ISBN: 9798863409092

No part of this book may be reproduced by any mechanical, photographic or electronic process or in the form of photographic recording; nor may it be stored in a retrieval system, transmitted or otherwise copied for public or private use-other than "fair use" as brief quotations embodied within. The intent of this author is only to offer information of general nature to inspire you on your spiritual journey and for personal growth.

The material contained in this book is only the opinion of the author and is not intended as medical advice. If you have a medical issue or illness, consult a qualified physician.

In the event you use any of the information in this book for yourself, the author and publisher assume no responsibilities for your actions.

Dedication

To my Auntie, a guiding light to thousands through example and who has inspired me and my entire life... and continues to do so to this day.

To "Mumzy" and Dad, the biggest providers of love and support... in mine and my children's life.

To my children who inspire me to keep trying to be a better version of myself, each new day.

To my partner, family and chosen family, my deepest gratitude.

Your unconditional support and love have assisted me to step into the place I am today, as I continue to practice and grow in this lifetime.

To all that have suffered and feel this hole within the soul, reach out, seek guidance, keep talking, keep healing and know that spiritual abundance is yours to have.

Preface from the author

As long as I can remember, I have been spiritually thirsty. I still have the Children's Bible my God-Mother, Auntie Bev, gave me, 40 plus years ago. I can't explain why or when the thirst started, I just always remember feeling as though there was something greater than me, than us, than this world.

My family wasn't a religious family. We didn't attend church every Sunday but my mother did teach my sister and I to say a prayer at a young age before sleep each night. *"Now I lay me down to sleep, I pray the Lord my soul to keep. If I should die before I wake, I pray the Lord my soul to take."* We would then say *"God Bless"* and list all the members of our family.

Looking back, seems pretty whack to pray about my soul, should I die in my sleep in the middle of the night, as a child. I wonder, if as a little girl, I ever worried about that? I don't recall.

I had an undeniable connection with my Auntie, my mother's sister. It wasn't the same connection as a mother and daughter, but equally and powerfully impactful. I was drawn to her like a moth to the flame. There was a familiar feeling that felt comfortable with her and I often recollect wanting more: more time with her, more conversations with her, and more connection to her.

As a little girl, I wanted to learn more about spirituality and God. When I was eight years old, I would get on a bus, head to church by myself on Sundays, waving bye to my family. They didn't want to go to church, but supported me in in my quest and desire to. One time, while my Auntie was visiting, she attended with me. We went to the big people's cathedral that day, where all the adults congregated. I was thrilled and excited and proud.

I normally had attended a group at the church for young gals such as myself called "Little Women". I can still hear the leader teaching us girls about hygiene, conservative hairstyles and make up and dressing appropriately, "in the eyes of God."

Not long after this life lessons, my family and I were out for pizza night. I excused myself to use the restroom and when I came out of the washroom stall, there was a woman putting lipstick on, in the mirror. She was beautiful. Lots of makeup, hair flowing long and her clothes were fancy. I couldn't help but notice her low cut blouse revealing her ample cleavage. As I washed my hands, gawking, she most likely felt my constant gaze and looked up at me and smiled as she walked out. I gasped. It was her. It was my church leader. All the things she told us not to do, she has done. It was my first taste of religious hypocrisy.

Years later in my adult life, my mother informed me that while I was attending this church at this young age, a representative of said church came to our home. They had informed my mom that while I attending this group, I had shared that my family loves to listen to music and dance around the house, that my parents' friends would come over and they would play guitar and sing and have drinks, while all the kids played in the rec room. Apparently, I shared that this was really fun and I loved it (because it was and I did). The lady at the door told my mother with concern that this was wrong and sinful. (I wonder if it was same woman at the pizza place?) My mom said she told the lady that is how we enjoy and celebrate life and there is nothing wrong with it.

I never knew why I stopped going to this church. I mean it made sense to me after my own experience of hypocrisy. As it turned out, my parents said it was enough.

Although I stopped going to church, I still enjoyed it from time to time. I craved a longing for connection and feelings of vitality that I felt satisfied when there, wherever there was.

I still maintained a relationship with God. I prayed and talked to the sky often as a child and soon learned I didn't need a building to have a spiritual connection.

Through the years, I read books and attended different churches, of varied religious philosophies.   As an adult, I started to have a realization that behind the history of religious wars and the dogmas and discussion of who was right and wrong, it was not religion that made me feel good. In fact, sometimes it made me feel bad.

Through hitting desperate bottoms in my adult life, I re-established my spirituality.   For me, God became an energy within me and each of us and also all around us. Spirituality had no rules, whereas religion felt based upon pre-established ritual and dogma. I felt a connection with myself and life on a soul level. I started to understand that we are these multi-layered, complex beings compiled of physical, mental, emotional, and spiritual layers and they are often very interconnected. I found that I could connect with this divine higher power and essence not only in the beautiful churches (which I still have an affection and penchant for) but at the beach, in the forest, in my home, in the yoga studio or wherever I am.

I began to recognize, it was spirituality, that lit up my soul. I knew that my allure to churches and readings of different religious doctrines was not the religion itself but the interconnectedness to something transcendent and bigger than me. I could feel the theme of spirituality woven in the various dogmas, opinions and beliefs, held by social group or religion. I came to understand that while spirituality may be present in religion, not all religious people lived a spiritual life and that spirituality was independent from religion.

For me spirituality and connection to a higher power, the divine or God, is an all-encompassing love that is the source and pulse of the universe. A source of energy beyond all of life while coincidingly indwelling within all life. God is everywhere. A spiritual energy of no denomination with non-judgmental love and acceptance. There are many paths to this connection, individual and extraordinary to each of us.

Spiritual living became my focus to find my contentment in life. I learned where I was powerless and where I was powerful. How to become the best version of me today, as I grow here, and how to connect with the world around me in all my interactions, both personally and professionally.

I sought for the meaning of life and how to maintain connection, rather than follow the rules, rites and rituals of man-made religion. I asked myself, how do I live the best way I can? Doing this based on my individual insights from seeking answers from within my soul, rather than from a particular group telling me what is true and right.

Daily living practices such as gratitude journaling along with spiritual routines such as yoga, mediation and time in nature, cultivated feelings of meaningful connection with something bigger than me, resulting in more positive emotions, such as peace, awe, contentment, immense appreciation, trust and acceptance.

The truth of the matter is I was a suffering soul at one point in my adult life and my Auntie, my

God-Mother was a guiding force to bring me to the life I live now. For years, she has held my hand through discussion to bring me back to my heart-centre. In fact, she has been a spiritual guide, through the Grace of God as she would say, for hundreds, if not thousands of people in the world.

Our stories are different, but parallel. My dear Aunt, now 90 plus years young, has shared her story with me and how she healed what she refers to as, the hole in her soul.

This is her story. A story that spans decades. A story of spiritual bankruptcy to spiritual abundance.

Chapter 1

The 1930's

The small village of Iroquois had everything a child would need growing up. I lived with my mom and dad, and when I was five, a little sister joined the family. Family was abundant where I lived.

My mom's parents, Grandma and Grandpa Deeks lived here and Great Grandma Deeks too. They lived together outside the village in the country, on a farm that overlooked the St. Lawrence River. Grandma Deeks's parents lived here also, right in the village. We called them Grandma and Grandpa Robertson. My mom's sister and brothers all resided in the Iroquois area: Aunt Mary, Uncle Donnie and Uncle Art.

My dad's family was not as abundant but still present. His father passed when he was just a little boy. I think it was from something with the heart but can't remember really. Dad had an older sister that lived out west along with Aunt Min, who married into prestige and money and lived on one of the most prominent streets in Vancouver. My dad also had twin siblings that both suffered from spina bifida and died quite young. When my dad was just a preteen, his mother, was admitted to the Ontario Mental Hospital. She died there, most likely from a broken heart from losing two children and a husband. I, therefore never met Grandma and Grandpa Brouse, but their siblings, my Uncle Don and his wife Emmy and Uncle John Brouse, all lived in the village or countryside nearby. After dad's mom passed, orphaned, Uncle Don and Aunt Emmy, along with the help of other families, took care of him.

No one ever talked openly about my dad's difficult childhood but I would find answers through my questions, to the grandmas.

Grandma Deeks always had a soft spot for my dad and felt sorry for him for not having any immediate family around.   She took him under her wing as if he was her own. His childhood story always made me sad.

I felt happy as a child but there was an unnamed thirst for more. More of what, I did not know.

That is until a woman we all called Aunt Ruby rolled into town with a car and guitar. Despite actually being no one's aunt, she landed in Iroquois,

Ontario, and brought her Angelical Pentecostal ways with her, which were all foreign to our small town. She rented a room at the front of a building and ran a religious summer school for kids. Aunt Ruby strummed her guitar while we all sang along with her. She taught us prayers and talked about God. Once. she somehow got some radio airtime in Brockville, a town nearby and had me singing hymns with her on the radio.

    I simply loved it all.

    Not everyone in our town was as overjoyed in doing this with Aunt Ruby, but I sure was. While I was familiar with church as our family attended the United Church, there was something I was drawn to in a new way. There was more action with Aunt Ruby and I loved all of that. I was always trying to get the other kids to join me at Aunt Ruby's place. As protestants, my Grandma and Grandpa Robertson were trying to keep me out of Ruby's grasp. I can't say specifically what it was but I knew I loved gathering in the groups together, singing hymns and having spiritual discussions. There was something about her that resonated with me, even at such a tender age.

I had a special affectionate bond with my father. My mother often said that all the extended family was so overly affectionate and attentive to me, that she needed to give more attention to my baby sister. Seemingly to me, my mother didn't offer me *any* affection. She offered loving care to my little sister but all my hugs and verbal praise came from others. I wasn't bothered by it as I was not short of any adoration I needed. From my father, aunts, uncles, grandparents, great grandparents, I received a lot of warmth, just not from my mother.

She was never cruel to me. She took care of me, provided for me. She did the physical tasks of dinner and laundry and so on. There was simply no attachment. Kind and providing, but not the same affection she gave to my younger sibling. I never felt she didn't love me; I simply had no connection with her. We had maids then, and I had a similar relationship to Jenny and Ruth, our maids, as I did my mother.

I don't ever remember being jealous of my sister. I didn't crave my mother's approval, after all, I had my dad. In fact, I never gave my mother's detachment from me, much thought. My father filled any potentially felt gap, with his loving endearment.

I loved going to work with him. He owned a car dealership and I remember him lovingly letting me sit on his lap as he moved the cars around the lot, pretending I was in the driver's seat. I wanted to be with him whenever I could.

The 1930's were an era where you had money or you were poor. Mother never worked, my father had several businesses and we had money. My father was quite successful for being only in his late 20's. My mother, the lady of the house didn't work but she was very busy. She enjoyed playing tennis and other athletics. Any club available, she was a part of. She volunteered with V.O.N., girl guides and other organizations and was an active member in our community.

I always was performing for someone, perhaps channeling my inner Ruby. One time my mother was in a musical play at the town hall and she often took me with her. I knew every one of the songs and all the people in the performance. After rehearsals and shows, we often went to the "Dainty Eat" restaurant, another one of my father's businesses. They would have me standing on the tables singing off all these songs, performing for everyone.

Sometimes after work, my dad would come home late with some of his car sales men for a dinner. I would already be in bed, but dad would wake me up to show me off. These men, certainly not interested in seeing a child perform anything, but they wanted my father to buy their cars for his lot, so I suppose they made a big fuss over me singing and dancing for them. Either way, I didn't mind performing and after all, it was for my dad and his hugs and kisses.

When I was seven years old, my life and all of our lives were altered in a way we didn't know the extent of, at the time. My father had gone to Toronto, Ontario, on and off for weeks, maybe months. Time was hard to track as a little girl.

One day, my two-year-old sister and I were sleeping in the room at the back of the house and when we woke, my father was standing there, in a crisp handsome uniform and he was saluting us. He had joined the Canadian Air Force.

For a while, my father was travelling back and forth to Toronto for training and when he would come home, he would pay me to shine and clean the brass buttons on his uniform. I didn't know what all this meant and didn't consciously miss him when he was gone but I always loved when he came home and I got to shine the buttons.

Eventually he travelled to Yarmouth, Nova Scotia to the Royal Air Force training base. While there, my mother was in a terrible car accident. She had gone off the road in grandpa Deeks's car and hit a tree. She had a lot of internal traumas; a broken back and ribs punctured her lungs. They thought she would die.

She survived but was in the hospital for several months. I don't remember worrying but I do recall all the adults worrying and being very sad for my mom, and *praying* for her. I was being kept care of by my great-grandparents in town. My sister was being taken care on the farm with grandma Deeks and family.

My father was transferred to a nearby Air Force base to be closer until she was no longer in danger.

My mom eventually healed well enough and went home to grandma Deeks's house with my sister to live. I stayed at various places around town such as my Aunt Mary's, Grandma Robertson and even my friends' parents, the Grisdale's, for a bit.

There was lots of family around, however, my Uncle Donnie was gone, my Uncle Art was gone and my adoring, loving father, was gone. They all joined the Air Force and were sent overseas to England and Belgium to fight in the war. We wouldn't see them again for five years.

Chapter 2

The 1940s

We lived in a big house in Iroquois. It was a lot for my mother on her own and difficult to heat in the winter due to its size. Consequently, every winter, my mother and my sister Anne, went down and stayed with Grandma and Grandpa Deeks on the farm. It was beautiful there. When you sat on their veranda, you looked out at the St. Lawrence River. After a few years, my sister eventually would go to the country school house in the winters, which taught all grades in one class. The same schoolhouse my mother and all my aunts and uncles went to.

While my mom and Anne were very connected, I was just floating around. I stayed in town with the great grandparents and continued at the same school.

Every spring and summer, we reopened our house and my sister and mother and I would all return back together in the family home. We repeated this routine every winter for the entire war. Despite not living on the farm, I had spent lots of time there and I enjoyed that. I have wonderful memories of podding peas with my great-grandma Deeks and getting vegetables ready- from farm to table. She was weak so she was always just sitting in the chair. She would do all the darning of socks, mending of clothes and prepare vegetables for dinner, basically anything you could do while sitting down in a chair.

    I don't remember missing anyone during the time on my own other than my father. I missed him terribly and wanted him home, but I was still happy. There were always people around and I think they were trying to make up for the fact that he was gone. There was a lot of family support.

    I felt like I was writing a new letter to send off to him overseas all the time, attempting to articulate to him just how much I missed him, like that would somehow bring him back.   I would be overjoyed if I received a letter back. Dad, often penning that he missed me too and reassuring me that he would be home soon. One time I sent him some Rice Krispies squares that I had proudly made. By the time they made their way to Europe, I'm sure they were harder than the bullets they were using over there.

The war wasn't just hard on those that went to war. It was also difficult on those left behind, waiting and wondering. It took its toll on the families, including my mother. She was lonely, it seemed. Life was hard for everyone; alone, missing, worrying or grieving.

However, I kept busy doing things I loved and I enjoyed helping others. I would help my grandma make baskets up for families. I would walk up and down the long farm house laneways and to nearby homes to deliver care packages.   I enjoyed assisting others with my grandma and this made me feel really good in my heart.

Often told, just how easy going I was and good natured, I embraced this whole-heartedly. I felt like I wanted to or perhaps felt it was necessary to communicate to everyone with a happy smile, that I was just fine and that life was sunny-side up. I developed an attitude, that I ought to be showing all that life is good and okay. My father had imparted on me that I was this happy little kid that everyone would want to see perform from the time I can remember. I soon felt that was my worth and what I had to be.

So, I was.

I developed or at least convinced myself to have a certain confidence as a young gal and excelled as such. In school I would be a part of all the oratorical contests, and I always got 100%. While all the other kids were faking sick and staying home as they were scared to death of getting up in public to speak, I could get up there, centre stage and rattle the speeches off with ease.

Over the few years of the war, I had lots of friends. I joined clubs. I spent life surrounded by many loving family members. The lessons from Aunt Ruby, church and others left me trying to be a good person and to be kind to others. All of this felt very good to me. People seemed to like me, which of course I thought, who wouldn't?

Grandpa Robertson died suddenly. He had a heart attack. I am not sure how old he was. Eight-something? The casket was brought to the big farm house for viewing and ceremony. I noticed my grandma didn't seem upset which was confusing, so I asked her. Grandma explained, "well he's just gone on, gone ahead and gone home to God." She told me when the time is meant, she would be with him again, someday. I thought it was a nice way to look at it. It felt comforting to me.

I was the happy little girl my father told me I was, I just didn't have my father. And while I missed him terribly, my mother seemed to be insensitive to this and there was never a discussion about it. Ever.

Several Years later ...

"THE WAR IS OVER" was blasting over the radio. It was May of 1945.

Once the announcement came, the soldiers were coming back quickly before the school year ended. My dad was being given the highest medal of honor for his bravery and outstanding service beyond the call of duty as a service officer in the war. The British Empire Medal was to be given to him by King George of England, but he would have had to stay until the end of the month and he wanted nothing to do with that. He was ready to come home. He did receive the medal, just not from his Majesty.

It was only a few weeks after we heard the good news, that the day had finally arrived. My father, my everything, was returning to me and I was simply over the moon.

My mother went to meet my dad in Montreal. Anne, now seven years old and myself, 12, were at Grandma Deeks in Iroquois, when we got the call. It was him. He was at Aunt Vera's, who now lived in Montreal. I was overjoyed and ecstatic to hear him, when I finally got to talk to him. I hadn't heard his voice or he mine, in half a decade. Dad asked us what we wanted, as he was going to buy us gifts while they were in the big city. My sister asked for a purse and I asked for a CCM bike, and we got just that when he finally arrived home.

When I first saw him, as a young preteen now, I was looking quite different, although he looked the same to me. He was also the same loving and affectionate father I remember. His hugs, were home to me.

The night he came home there was a big parade. The town brought out the big fire trucks to give the returning soldiers a proper celebration when each of them returned home. My dad was a very well-known business man in town before the war, so there were lots of people out to welcome him home. The town folks were applauding and cheering. It was such a wonderful moment for everyone, but especially for me.

The fire truck drove through the town and it stopped in front of the Bank, the only bank in our town, and all the people in the town were out to talk to him and "Bob", another returning soldier.

My dad, Cormack, often shortened his name to Mac. He was a tall man. Everyone often talked about how big Mac was. Dad in his uniform, looking so tall and handsome got out to talk to everyone that had come to celebrate. I was so very proud of him for having been in the war, and for winning this special award by the Royals of England and this celebration. It was one of those nights that I will never forget.

Mom, Anne and I were all back into the family home as it was spring and now my dad was home, too. He was back and I never wanted him to leave me again.

He was a little lost though, as many of the returning soldiers were. He had sold all his businesses to join the war. There was talk of what he would do, what businesses he would open or if he would continue with the Air Force or policing.

He did some odd paint jobs with a couple of men but nothing permeant, for some time.

No one returning from war was themselves anymore. The experiences that any of these men had, were never ever discussed. We lived not far from the highway in our big house and as the transport trucks drove by, they would occasionally backfire and my father would literally jump out of his chair in alarm.

My dad was a stranger to my sister, after all, she was only two when he left and now, she is seven. She didn't really want anything to do with him and they didn't really get along, as such. He may not have been the same man, but he was the same father to me and he was good to me and I loved him dearly and simply couldn't be happier for his return. I didn't want to leave his side. Where he went, I wanted to go.

There was not the same enthusiasm in my parents' relationship.

My mom and dad were not getting along at all, fighting often. The years apart, as well as the post-war effects on my dad, were apparent in their relationship.

Soon, dad went to Quebec to a rehabilitation centre for soldiers for what seemed liked weeks. They didn't really know what was wrong with him or give it a title, but many soldiers were afflicted the same way.

The time dad spent at the Vets centre apparently didn't go well. They tried to teach him how to knit and he fired the knitting needles across the ward room. If you knew my dad, the last thing that he would have found to be therapeutic or beneficial was knitting. So, he left the centre and came home.

Not long after my dad returned home again, my parents fighting continued and my dad was feeling without purpose of a job or business. At some point, it was decided, my parent would separate.

My mom wanted my sister to be with her, and they would go and live with my Aunt Mary and Uncle Hubert. My dad wanted to keep me with him. I remember feeling a little sorry for my mother as I had this strong connection with dad and she didn't really have much say in the matter of where I would go. Although she had her Annie.

Dad's aunt and sister, that lived out west, decided dad needed to focus on building a career again. It was resolved that I would go live in Vancouver, British Columbia with them while he got his footing again.

Despite the family separation and my dad's situation, this young teen thought it was very exciting to be travelling the world.

I had done some travelling in Ontario, as every summer since I was about 5 years old, I would go to Aunt Vera's house where ever she was living: Ottawa, Brockville, Kingston and Montreal. This was bigger though. I was travelling to the other side of the country and I was too busy feeling good and having fun, to worry about any of that other stuff.

Dad and I drove to Montreal where I met some of his family that lived out that way. My Uncle Win was in the city on business and he and I would travel by train together, back to British Columbia. Uncle Win (short for Winston) was a Wing Commander in the Canadian Air Force. One time there was the "meeting of the Win's", as my family jokingly referred to it. At the base, Uncle Win received the honor of meeting Sir Winston Churchill, a British statesman who served as Prime Minister of the United Kingdom from 1940 to 1945.

Uncle Win and I had a compartment on the train and it was all very exciting and sensational. Although I would miss my dad, I was thrilled to go live with dad's sister, my Aunt Marie. Our wealthy great Aunt Min, had decided she would be paying my way to attend a private boarding school for girls. I felt very special, indeed.

My easy-going nature and confidence allowed me to make friends and get along just fine while I lived in Vancouver and I was having a wonderful time.

While I was away, apparently my parents had reconciled and packed up and moved with my younger sister. They had sold our home in Iroquois and bought a place in St. Catherine's and dad opened some billiard halls for business.

It was as if I was a rubber ball and now this ball was bouncing again. They had been living there for many months and now, they wanted me back home, so home I came after a year or so in Vancouver.

The train arrived in Toronto at the Union Station, my mom and sister came to pick me up. I hopped off that train and my sister swiftly ran to me and gave me the biggest hug. She was so happy to see me and it felt good as I was happy to see her too. My mother contrastingly, showed little or no emotion nor did she hug me. Mind she never ever hugged and kissed me as a child, so why would this be different. Regardless, it was good to be back.

I started high school in St. Catherine's with ease. It was effortless for me to talk to people and because I was good at sports, I would just join the various teams.

However, the next year in 1948, we moved to Galt. I never really felt strange or bad, I was just moving around and meeting new people, so it seemed to me.

Within a year of going to my new school in Galt, I had made wonderful friends; the kind of friends that would last my life time. I was Captain of the basketball and volleyball team, the Posture Queen, a cheerleader, and joining this club and that group. I had the attention of lots of boys and at the school dances they were lining up to dance with me. I had great friends and we were in a little bit of clique. I suppose we were in the popular crowd, but I also had a couple of young, less "in" crowd kids telling me once, that they really liked me as I was kind and friendly to them, not like other popular snobs that would just walk by.

My mother and father had announced they had conceived another child and my mother was going to be having another baby. Bowling Alleys were just becoming a big thing and my dad had opened some bowling alleys in Galt. My parents seemed happy.

My dad had his businesses again. My little sister was now ten and I had another sibling was on the way. I loved school and my friends.

Life, was exciting.

Chapter 3

The 1950s

My baby brother was born but there were complications. He was diagnosed with Dwarfism. Dr. Howell was trying to help my brother, now two years old and made a specialist referral. My mom and dad were busy taking him to Sick Kids Hospital in Toronto, frequently.

I still hung with the same gals and I was still loving all the sports and clubs and other social groups of high school. I believe I was kind to all and I continued to have a very friendly nature to all the kids at my school. No one felt superior or inferior to me. Despite my popularity, I don't believe I was conceited or elevated by it.

By the time I was a senior at high school, I occupied the interest of many young men. Jim, who had been going to Rigley College for boys, had a back issue, so he came home to Galt for treatments. While being treated he went to Galt Collegiate High School. He was tall and handsome and had a couple of cars. He was very attractive to me. There was also Benny, who was a square kind of guy and went onto be a lawyer. I had lots of friends that were boys too. Fact be, I seem to enjoy male companionship over female, although I did have some great gal pals.

Another boy that pursued my affection was Ken Thomson. His father was a millionaire, Lord Thomson that owned a chain of publications. He was working at the Galt Reporter and was always trying to get me to go out with him or pay attention to him and he would bring me back gifts from Europe after he was jet-setting. However, I thought he had too many grey flannel suits and grey oxfords, and I wasn't so interested in that. It didn't impress me much. I liked jeans and sneakers and jocks and had my heart set on someone else.

I was 18, when I met a wonderful jock. His name was Don but his sister's friends thought he was so sweet, that his nickname by them and soon, from all, came to be, Sugar. He was fun, popular and out-going. I got myself a real catch.

I was still adoring and wanting to please my father; however, I was a young woman now, so I wanted to please him only if it worked for me. Dad had aspirations for me to continue my education and go onto to university. Instead, I choose marriage.

I remember our wedding day in 1953. We both knew lots of people, so leaving the church, folks were lined up the street outside, waving and we were waving back, like we were king and queen of the town.

Externally, life was pretty darn good. I was liked, I had my family, a new husband and I was unaware of anything beyond that.

Internally, there was a latent, slow decline in my emotional maturity. There was a whispering soul sickness within me, I was completely oblivious too. It was there, but I didn't feel it, see it, or acknowledge it. I just kept living life.

My great friend Audrey also got married. She seemed to be settling down, not going out partying and living it up or going out to places all the time. Her husband and her weren't spending money they didn't have. They started saving and being mature young adults.

That was not Sugar and I. We were unknowingly, a couple of immature kids playing house, after the wedding ceremony. Sugar, or as I and most call him now, D.R., was the life of the party while seeking and getting lots and lots of attention. We didn't seem to be doing the same as my friend Audrey, and I didn't give it much thought.

My father was still a big supporter of me and often spoiled me. My new husband and I lived in a house my father bought me. When D.R. was busy living it up instead of paying for things, he was supposed to be paying for, like house bills or the car, my father paid for it. Dad bitched about it, but he always stepped up and paid for it, for me. I often felt that no matter what, if not my husband or my father, someone would be looking after me.

We got caught up in the social life. D.R. was, who he was, always seeking the spot light, and being funny, and he was funny, but that there was not much more than that beneath that surface. I noticed others would think of me as perhaps the more mature one of this coupling, giving innuendos that I as stuck with him. As much as I would like to believe that, within me somewhere, I knew I was not emotionally mature either, whether I acknowledged that or not. But none the less, life kept moving along.

The following year, I entered a new role in my life. Motherhood. I had my first child; a boy named Rick.

The social scene didn't let up for D.R. He stopped at the nearby hotel each night after work to drink, some nights later than others. There was the men's room, where no women were allowed, and then there was a couple's room, where women could attend. This was not unusual for many men to attend after work. Not my friend Audrey's husband Roger though; he matured. D.R. did not and this became our way of life.

D.R. was working for Turnbull Textiles company and was transferred to the Toronto office. We packed up the house and our little boy and moved to Willowdale. My dad felt sorry for me being there all by myself as a young mother so he bought me a big television and TV stand. We were not there long, less than a year and Turnbull's transferred D.R., back to Galt. My father was building homes at this point and we moved back to where my family lived, moving into one of dad's new homes.

When we moved into this new place, my dad purchased us a washer and dryer, so that I didn't have hang my clothes on the line. Folks often teased me about being "daddy's little girl" despite being a young mother in my twenties. I didn't mind a bit.

When I was 23 years old, I had my sweet daughter Cathy. At the same time, my father had a stroke. He had an operation and was hospitalized for a short while. Weak and unable to talk properly, he wasn't able work for some time after being released home. We were still living in the house my dad gave me and my parents only lived a few blocks away from us. During this time, my dad would come over every single morning, and we would watch game shows on the television, as he needed something to do and keep him busy. Our connection was as strong as it ever was and we spent a lot of time together with my young kids, during this period. I was happy spending my time with him and I was happy being mother.

My sister had just left high school and started working while still living at home with our parents. My mother was playing in a bridge group as well as bowling, golfing and curling, after getting the house work done (which she was never fond of doing). She was slightly more affectionate with my children, than I remember she was to me as a child. Perhaps it was the role of being a grandmother, I suppose. I never did develop a stronger relationship with her and it just didn't seem to matter. I had my dad.

My friends, Audrey and Roger bought a house from my dad and lived across the street, with their little girl, Brenda. The adults were often hanging out with each other while the kids played together.

Superficially, life was pretty darn good.

My relationship with my husband was not what I would have wanted it to be though and we were growing apart. I was a young mother and I kept busy. In the neighborhood, I ran around trying to do nice things for people. I was making and handing out casseroles to folks, trying to show everyone that I was a-okay.

I knew, I was not.

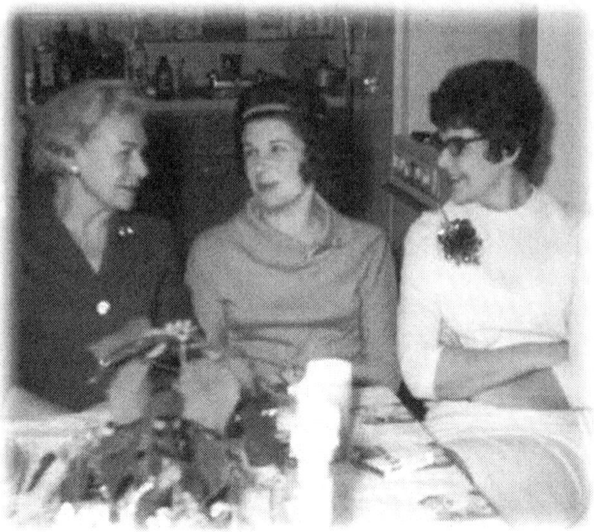

Chapter 4

The 1960s

D.R. was doing his own thing in life, while I was taking care of our little kids. If our hydro wasn't being turned off, then our phone was being disconnected.

He was not taking responsibility to pay our bills and rent despite working full time and at a good job. Who knows where all the money went? No one could figure it out. I just knew, my dad was always rescuing us. I would let my dad know what was going on, and he would make sure things stayed hooked up.

We were seemingly not mature enough to be dealing with our problems in a respectful and responsible way. We were living in the same house but separate. When we were alone, there was a thick tension, conversation ceased and we were no longer talking. It was a terrible time and no way to live. We slept in the same bed but intimacy was non-existent. I felt tense, all the time.

I never talked to him about the problems. Fact was, you simply couldn't have a serious conversation with D.R. He couldn't with anyone, anytime, ever. But he was the life the party and he was playful with the kids, as he was a big kid himself. I clearly wasn't mature enough to recognize that this was not enough or this would be the way I wanted my life.

I craved more.

There was such a lack of attention from my husband. As such, I developed a closer relationship with one of our friends, Dave, that was often around. He and I always got along just fine and I could talk to him. But our relationship advanced much further than it should have, for two married people. It was obvious that he cared for me a lot and so, it didn't bother me so much that my husband, from my empty marriage, would not be okay with this. Instead, I became more interested in the attention I was getting, rather than the lack of attention I was not receiving.

My life became a very superficial way of living. I couldn't have articulated it at the time but I knew there was more than this. I knew my soul craved to communicate in deeper spiritual talks beyond social gatherings, discussions about children and what we were baking that day. I subconsciously felt this faint, deep need within me, that was unchecked. I never talked to anyone about this, nor would I know what to say about this spiritual thirst, I just knew it was there.

I continued this close relationship with Dave, despite knowing that this was unacceptable. There was a lot wrong with my marriage and my husband certainly had his faults, but I can not blame D.R. for the way I was behaving.

I felt great shame, remorse and immense guilt. I was being something I should not be and behaving in ways I should not be behaving, but I didn't have any solution for it, at this time, anyway.

There was no escape from the way I was feeling, and no one I could talk to about it, so I stuffed those dark, negative emotions down deep and I began a slow paralysation into fear. My life was a lie. I was not allowing myself to be honest and was not living honestly, to myself or to anybody. I had become a living contradiction, to what my inner beliefs were and who I thought I was.

My marriage ended in 1960. D.R. and I were still living together but living separate. I was still talking to Dave frequently and would go and meet him outside the home. Although I did not do anything to prevent this marital catastrophe, the final blow came from my estranged husband.

On this particular night, I had come home after being out. I couldn't get into the house. I tried, but my keys wouldn't work. D.R. had changed all the locks on the doors. I knew things were absolutely terrible but I didn't see this coming. It was never a thought that this would happen, especially since I was locked out of the home that my father owned and paid for, for me.

I was in utter disbelief. My kids were inside, D.R. was inside and I was standing outside, alone.

The devastation was festering rapidly. The loss was malignant. I blamed myself and the self-loathing of my role in this was crushing. I was no longer living a life that I yearned for, ignoring the deep needs within my soul.

As long as I can remember, I had attempted to live a spiritual way of life, with ethics and values of what I was taught. I could not believe what I had done and what I had done to my children. There was a hole in me now and this was the beginning of the breakdown of my spiritual integrity and my inner principles. I could no longer be honest to anyone about how I was living, as I knew it was wrong. I certainly could not have described it as a soul sickness, but it was. Instead, I solely felt like a bad, bad person. I felt sinful.

Despite the shame I felt for the way I had acted; I was also ashamed to be a divorced woman in a time where that was unique and a big, big deal. It appeared to many that my husband was the bastard and bad guy. I suppose I liked that part, to ease my own inner demons. But I knew I was incapable of dealing with anything above the neck and I was aware that I could have done things far, far differently. I wanted to believe their blame of him, but I couldn't and I didn't. I became more conflicted.

I moved home with my parents and younger brother and sister. My father thought I could have tried or worked harder or something. I think he just didn't want me to be separated. I had to make money for myself, so I got a job at the nearby hotel.

Shortly after my move back to parents' home, a taxi arrived. D.R. had put what little belongings I had, my clothing and personal possessions, in a taxi cab and sent them to my parents. My dad was furious. He didn't confront my husband but rather went and talked to D.R.'s parents, with little to no success. My mother, while seemingly fairly supportive of me, didn't want any part of being involved in the mess, so it wasn't discussed much. My parents upset, only adding to my own shame and loathing.

D.R.'s mother and father moved into the house to take care of Rick and Cathy, when he was at work. All these years, I did not have job, as I had been taking care of my kids that were now four and six. As well, most women didn't work. My dad got me a lawyer. We had papers drawn up and got a separation and custody agreement. Because of the situation the way it was, the children would stay with their dad and grandmother and I would get visits.

But as it often goes, in difficult endings, with difficult feelings experienced by each, everything was a fight. Each interaction we had, was volatile and difficult and it made it next to impossible to follow the agreements that were set forth. Custody visits were not adhered to, nor were they possible, due to the pain within and between, both of us.

The gossip and lies swirled in our small town. Some folks picked sides, as they do. My friend Audrey attempted to remain neutral after all, she lived across the street from them and the kids played. I respected that about her. Her neutrality came to a halt though when she was told blatant lies about me that she knew could not be true. For a fleeting moment, I didn't feel the pit of pain, with her support. It didn't last however.

Mrs. Town was supporting her son, and was pretty underhanded about it all, feeding into. But my ex-father-in-law, Mr. Town wrote me a letter to tell me how terrible he thought it all was. It made me feel a little bit like there was some understanding of the truth, but the shameful embarrassment remained strong.

Despite having joint custody, the arrangements were not upheld regardless of any of my efforts. I didn't get to see my children very much. Interactions during visitation exchanges, always had unattainable stipulations or challenging rules. It was very chaotic for the kids and it broke my heart.

When I did get to visit them, my son was a busy boy and he didn't seem to be affected, as much. He liked my brother Donnie and they would often play together and enjoy each others company, after all, they were only a handful of years in difference and my brother was small like Rick, due to his dwarfism. My sweet Cathy, at the tender age of four, however, did not fair as well. She wanted to be with her mother. I never knew what to say to her, as she was only four. She was often very upset and sad. I just did my best to let her know, how much I loved her and cared about her.

This caused me to feel more pain, more guilt and more shame. It distressed and troubled me immensely, to see my children go through any of this. I always wanted to protect them and despite my best efforts to keep connection with them, I felt that I had failed them.

The hopelessness I felt was awful and astounding. I never talked about any of this, other than the superficial details, with a single person.

The spiritual disease within me, began to snowball.

Over the next couple of years, the shame I felt within myself, which is also what I thought others felt towards me too, remained but quietened a little. Up until this point in my life, I had lived a good life. I had received a lot of adulation and praise for my schooling and sports, then my marriage and so on. I could delicately feel how I used to feel, but knew I would never feel the same. The shame remained.

In 1962, Dave and I, got married. The following year, we moved to the city of London, as Dave's work relocated him there. Many friends thought this was perhaps, a good idea to get out of Galt. We would drive the one-hour distance back and forth to get my children for visits.

We bought a new house that I just loved. It wasn't a big, fancy house but the perfect house full of character. We made new friends. I got a new job. No one knew about me and what happened. No one knew about the two kids that I saw so rarely because of the circumstances.

It was a fresh start. I was feeling okay.

Two years later, Dave and I have a boy together and we named him David. One would think, I would be content with this new beginning, with a wonderful man, a new child, in a new city, and with a new life. I thought everything would be just fine now.

But the hole in my soul, was not filled. I may have left the village where the troubles happened, but I took them with me and I am still caught-up on the shame and guilt, within me

Increasingly, I began to feel restless, irritable and discontented. I didn't know why, I just was.

The darkness within me would overshadow anything that was new, fresh and good in my life. At my job, the flattery I would receive from men telling me how wonderful I was, became comforting. I began drinking alcohol more. I mean everyone drank, but I was drinking more, for me. Many folks drank as much or even more than I was, but they didn't' have the soul sickness that I had and was blind to, at the time. People didn't tell me I had a drinking problem or anything but they sure thought I could drink. I remember my husband saying things like "don't try and keep up with Bev, she could drink you under the table." But they didn't carry the same remorse, shame, guilt and pain that I did, when they drank.

I was no longer content to stay home with my husband and David, now a toddler. I craved the parties and where the action was, where I would get attention and comfort, from other men. Lying about everything, became a way of living for me. Rather than living the way I knew I should be, the shame and guilt remained hidden in my shadows and I began to seek someone and something to fill the hole in my soul. In turn, I only amplified my inner pain.

I would look at myself in the mirror, crying, with these two eyes that were now just two holes in my head, with no expression whatsoever, and I would wonder, "what ever happened to the Bev that used to be?"

My boss at work told me that Dave had called him and said he was coming down to talk to me. Dave was a mild mannered, quiet man and I knew if he was coming to talk to me that there was something terrible had happened. I could tell by the way he was acting it was something major. Then he told me.

It was 1966, my mother had just undergone some back surgery. On a follow up appointment at the doctor's office, she passed a clot to her brain, had a massive stroke and died very quickly and tragically. I think it bothered him more to tell me, that it seemed to be in my reaction to it all. I never had an emotional connection with my mom, so my emotional response was seemingly parallel.

Mom was only 53 years old. I returned to Galt and did a lot of the planning. My dad sat there quietly as usual. My sister and brother were very emotional and distraught. My sister Anne, had just told her she was pregnant the night before with her second child. I put the funeral all together, while my Aunt Mary wondered how I did it all, so calmly.

I often used my mothers sudden passing for a reason for emotional instability and behavior, despite the truth of it all.

In 1968, my father and I travelled to British Columbia. Aunt Marie had passed young, from a sudden heart attack. I didn't have an overly strong emotional response to her passing. I wanted to travel with my dad and be there with him.

During that trip, I felt differently about my drinking. At the post-funeral gatherings, while family was all around, I had a conscious whisper of awareness, that I was not drinking the same. I had always drunk beer and this time, I drank rye, which I didn't even like.

I returned home to my job at car dealership. I got along just fine with this group.   They put me at the front desk where they thought I could charm the folks paying their service bills, that were being taken to the cleaners with overcharges. They always charged so much more than the little mechanic on the corner. They would joke, "send Bev to talk to them", because I usually could charm them with my friendly demeanour.

There was a crew of car people that were partiers. Not all, but generally it was party time. This was right down my alley. They were crazy funny, mocking each other and playing out silly antics. I thought they were more damn fun than a barrel of monkeys.

Initially I would work my evening shift and go home in decent time, as Dave was home taking care of David. But eventually, the evening shifts from four to nine p.m. got longer, the drinks more plenty and I began to get in more trouble with my behavior.

Often the next day at work, the other women, some single and some married, would be laughing about the indiscretions of the previous evenings party events. Despite having participated in at the time, there was nothing about it that I found funny about others' behaviors or my own. I didn't think it was funny at all and I could barely talk about it. I wanted to forget. I knew it was wrong for respectable married adults to be behaving like this. Without a doubt, I knew it was morally unacceptable. I was shocked with the lack of moral consciousness they all had or seemed to have, while I was riddled with remorse, shame and guilt. It didn't mean I stopped though. I wanted to, but for some reason I could not.

Friends of ours the Kerr's, owned a place up north in the Muskoka's, up near Zephyr Island. We all headed there and took the children. Dr. Wareing had a place up there too, so we had that in common. He was my obstetrician that delivered my youngest child, David. He thought I was such an upbeat, happy and joyful woman, as my personality was and where I felt my worth resided. Dave had talked to him, in concern, about my drinking and behavioral issues. He knew me and liked me and had a hard time believing what Dave had told him. Dave assured him that he would assist the doctor to believe, by inviting him over one night, when I was passed out under the dining room table.

Dr. Wareing called me and told me I should try and drink differently. He also referred me to a psychiatrist by the name of Dr. Down. But he might have well of sent me to a garbage collector, as I just told Dr. Down whatever-the-hell I felt like telling him, and whatever popped in my head, including reasons such as the "sadness" of my mothers sudden passing and the pain I carried from my poor two children that got lost in a bitter divorce. It seemed to me that was good material to share and he tried to help me from this perspective.

While the agony of circumstances around my children were certainly true, my mother had nothing to do with my turmoil. I was struggling with the fear of my father ever discovering the way I had been behaving, as disappointing him would be more than I think I could handle. I always wanted him to believe what he thought I was, rather that the truth of what I truly was.

For a while, I was pulling it off everywhere. Making friends, meeting neighbors, and being social with lots of people including those at my new job at the car dealership. I was pulling it off with those on the outside. I was covering up my pain, lying about the way I was living and some days I believed the crap I was telling others.

Home was a different story. My husband knew there was a problem. At times, I would drink a tumbler full of rye, pounding it back so fast that I would asphyxiate. Dave would hammer on my back to assist, as I simply couldn't breathe.

On some level, I knew within my soul, I was living a life that seemed to be out of control and when I drank, I would forget what was happening. I knew it was not good. I knew I was living in a way that was a contraction to my deepest spiritual needs. But nothing I tried to do, helped me to stop.

Over the next year or so, my spiritual disease progresses. I was lost. My drinking and unethical behavior had spiralled. I was breaking down at a rapid pace and in a very short period of time. I ended up several times, being admitted to psychiatric wards or psychiatric hospitals, where not one second of time there gave me any help or resolution. Often arriving in slippers, an orange and white housecoat and a red wig in a state of dishevelment.

Although I would cry leaving my little boy each time, I liked it once I was admitted to these institutes or wards. I was glad. I liked being in the hospital. Oddly, I escaped my craziness when they put me in a place for crazy people. It got me away from the mess I was creating out there beyond the walls of the hospital. Within a day or two after admission, I would be sobered up and looking and feeling like a million bucks, while running around telling everyone in there what they should be doing with their lives. I would become a self-declared occupation therapist and take them down to the sewing room and teach everyone how to make housecoats!

One time, after a binge and during one of my visits to the St. Joseph's psychiatric wards for my behaviors, a woman there was talking about her husband and his drinking. "One is too many and a thousand isn't enough". I thought that's a funny expression.

Meanwhile, I am in the place, because it applies to me. I was never in there long. Sister

Mary Margaret, a nurse on the ward, once said to me "The problem with you Mrs. Thomson is get yourself well, too fast." I thought she was nuts, after all, isn't that what you are suppose to do? But she was right. I would be in the hospital, sober up, appear more presentable and okay, and then be discharged quickly, only to repeat it again and again.

It was madness.

The doctors and nurses would tell me to slow down with the drinking. They medicated me full of valium and other drugs, while I was hospitalized. I can't remember what they would diagnose me with, depression, psychosis, who knows, I was in a haze. They would say "you can drink, just slow down" and then send me home with bags full of pills: pink ones, blue ones, yellow ones, white ones, you name it.

Time and again, I would leave these places and return to my restless, irritable, shameful and unmanageable ways.

The drinking had increased more and more, as was my lying. You couldn't trust a thing I said or did. The hopelessness intensified. I would often wonder, how much longer I would have to live this way. I was in complete conflict and contrast from the values and principles from who I was and how I wanted to be living and knew I should be.

I wasn't a daily drinker, so on the weekends that Rick and Cathy came to visit, I could usually pull it together enough. But on another given day, when David was at the babysitters, I would head over to the market, buy some cheap wine, drink out of the bottle and go into the bathroom stalls. I would sit on the john, with one foot up to hold the door closed because the latch was broken. The other stalls cost ten cents, which I didn't have. In there, I'd suck the bottle down, while crying and thinking, "if my grandmother could only see me now." I would want to try and control it or do it differently, but always wound up drinking myself to oblivion, simply to escape the reality of my life, that I had created.

Everyone would tell me to slow down and pace my drinking. I didn't think there was a drinking problem, or at least I tried to believe that. It was a remedy for me to quiet the beasts that dwelled in my soul, caused by the shame from the way I had lived and was currently living.

I had developed a mental obsession to find relief. All I could think about was drinking to pass out.

I was beginning to be a recluse. Part of the reasoning for isolating from others, is I could no longer pull off my happy, upbeat personable side of myself. The happy, little girl that entertained everyone was diminished and lost in the fog. I could no longer be what I thought people expected and valued me, to be. So, I would cancel events or simply not show up. My whole life, I had been an outgoing, extrovert by nature and now I just became someone that wanted to be left alone. Anybody that tried to show me compassion or kindness, I rejected it.

No matter how much unwarranted blame and anger I directed at Dave, I respected him. As much as a fog as I was in, I also knew he was such a good father to our son, David. I knew my husband was a man of integrity and despite my erratic, chaotic behavior, I was numbed out and I didn't pay much attention to how he was feeling.

My whole family was talking to me about my behavior and why don't I just straighten up. I knew hundreds of women that drank lots, including women in my family. I irrational thought "who the hell are they to tell me?" Or why did I have to go through all this? Why me?" Even, my beloved father would say to me "why are you drinking the way you are drinking, when you know what it's doing to your family?"

I had no answer.

In fact, I didn't know anybody else like me. Everyone drank, but not like me. No one else was behaving like me or neglecting life as I was.

This only amplified my inner turmoil and festering feelings of guilt and shame and anguish about everything - everything I had done years ago, everything I was doing now.

The days blurred and ran into one another. I was in a constant haze of intoxication or recovery from intoxication. Wandering the streets sometimes, contemplating with hopelessness and despair, *how long will this go on?*

I was spiritually bankrupt.

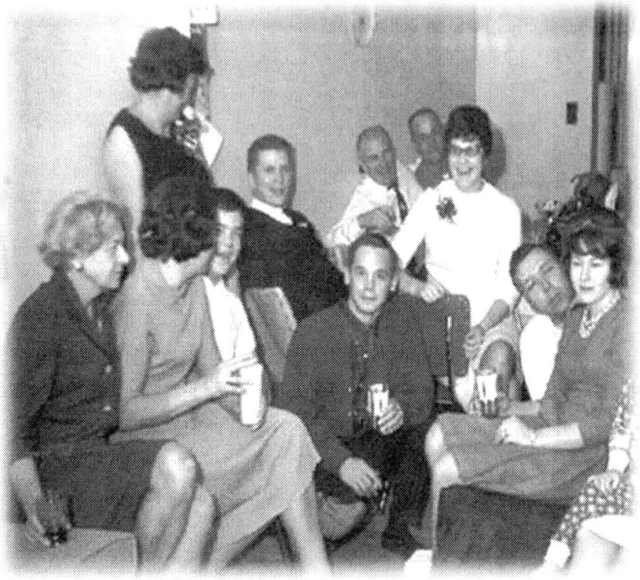

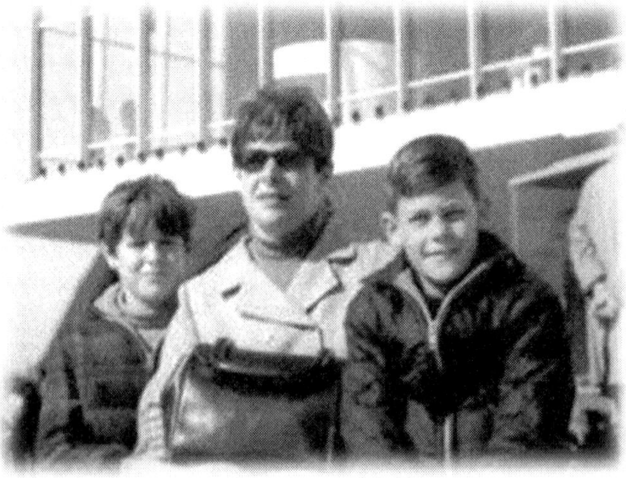

Chapter 5

The 1970s

It was December of 1970, just before the holidays. I was floundering in a deep pit of despair. I was admitted to a psychiatric hospital, again. The same patterns repeated, the same half truths and lies told, the same medications given and soon to be sent home.

I tried my best to behave. The Christmas Holidays were here, family was coming, and my little David, now six years old, so I really wanted to be good. I went through the motions of the holidays, a little numb. No one offered me a drink and I didn't drink in front of anyone. But I snuck and I hid. It was an internal jungle, to say the least.

For the first couple months of 1971, I honestly felt I was doing okay. I was still drinking. I was buying it and hiding it around the house, trying to control how much, when and where etc. I attempted to control it and change and find solution. I was a binge drinker, not a daily drinker, so as long as I could try my best to not overdo it, I thought I would be okay.

Then, I wasn't.

It was a bad one, this binge.

Dave had gone to the parent-teacher meeting without me. It was revealed that our son David, was having problems at school. The teacher told him, that David was misbehaving, appeared troubled by something and was attention seeking, while in the classroom. Dave confirmed to the teacher, that there was a problem and he was looking to eliminate that problem. What he really meant; he was looking into getting rid of me.

Dave was at his limit. He knew there was something wrong with me more than depression or whatever the doctors had labelled my behavior as. He went to the library and looked up "alcohol". He then reached out to Addiction Research Foundation, a centre for addictions and mental health. He read about "alcoholism". He researched and read and gathered information.

Then he came home to me, and said "I am sorry you are sick with alcoholism. But I am now aware, there is help for you and if you are not prepared to do something about it, we are not prepared to live this way anymore."

I had never heard the word alcoholism. It was not mentioned by any doctor or psychiatrist. This was the first time I heard of drinking alcohol as a disease. Never had one person told me to stop drinking, but to only drink differently.

I was not overly happy with Dave's proclamation, but I knew I didn't want to lose another child. I had to do this for my little boy and for my marriage.

So, I got help.

On Tuesday March 2, 1971, I found a spiritual recovery program for alcoholism, by the Grace of God. Dave dropped me off at the nearby Church for the group gathering in the basement there.

When it was over, I couldn't tell you what words were spoken at that recovery program, but I could tell you how I felt. I felt I belonged. People were smiling and people laughing. Someone told me I had a beautiful smile, which would have been plastered on my face as phony as a three-dollar bill, as my life was a mess. But they all seemed like they were doing okay. I wanted that.

I never drank another drink after this day.

I experienced the power of this spiritual program from that meeting at the first taste. While some others would express that it was hard to keep coming back regularly, I could hardly wait to return. Eager, I would be getting ready in the afternoon for an evening recovery meeting. I would read and practice what I would say to others, in my head. The feelings I were feeling were fresh, new and full of potential. I was feeling very good.

Less than a week after my first meeting, the co-founder spotted me from the get go and knew I needed a spiritual mentor or someone to guide me, support me, and direct me and to offer accountability. He told me there was a woman in the program, that he thought would be very good for me and asked if I would be willing to talk to her. This stranger gave me Geri's number and I called her and we set up a time to meet. Before we hung up, she asked me if I had any plans to drink, to which I thought, if I did you would be the last person I would want to be meeting with. I politely said no, I wouldn't do that.

We met. I left with appreciation for her. From our discussions, I respected her. She had a beautiful apartment on Richmond St. with beautiful furniture, from her family's antique store in the city. Her daughter, who was in university, came into the room singing, preparing for her graduation in Ottawa. I was impressed with all the surface things, I suppose. But also, I was attracted to what she had and represented. I liked being with her and felt good talking to her. I couldn't recognize what it really was, but I wanted to be like she was and aspired to attain the same spiritual level, she was living.

I continued to go to the recovery meetings regularly. I knew there was something there that kept me wanting more. I wasn't completely sure what they were all talking about usually but I did know that they showed interest in me, they would call and they were kind. I had been so off-track and there was still so much unresolved within me and I couldn't really identify the level of damage to my spirit yet, but the fog was starting to lift.

One thing, that I did hear them say was, that I had to have the willingness to do what I must do, to have what they had and to stay sober. I did not know what that all really meant, but I did pray, and ask for the willingness to do what must be done, to be like these people.

Some folks rejected the idea of prayer, or God, but I did not. They didn't want anything to do with it due to past religious challenge or over-intellectualization, despite it not being a religious group, but a spiritual one. Sometimes, very smart folks afflicted with alcoholism, had a harder time following the suggestions, as they lacked the humility to surrender and listen. Some folks didn't have any experience with praying, but were willing to do so and had faith in the advice from others. Perhaps from my upbringing or maybe the influence from the likes of "Aunt" Ruby and going to church, I am not sure, I just knew I did not have a problem with praying to the God of my understanding and I had faith and a willingness to follow through.

I had an arrogance in my thoughts. I have no idea why. Could be from confidence in my younger years. I had thoughts that I could figure out this recovery and how to heal myself with ease as well, be able to help others and get everyone else on track. I never thought this spiritual recovery program wouldn't work. Somehow, I knew it would. I simply thought I would get it all figured out in a hurry.

My love for the meetings and the way I felt had me happy and bouncing all over the place, helping out where I could. I received a lot of praise from others, telling me how good I was doing since arriving on the door steps of this recovery program. Mostly men, since there weren't many women in this program, at this time. This played well for my ego but not so great for my spiritual recovery, especially given my response to flattery in the past.

Fortunately for me, I had been partnered with a more experienced woman, well into her recovery, getting sober in 1956. If I didn't have Geri, as strong as she was and as willing to say the things to me that I probably wouldn't like (but needed to hear), I would have been in trouble. My ego-self, would often think, that when she learns how smart I really am, she won't be saying all this dumb stuff to me. But I was used to hiding my true feelings and was phony enough that I would just let-on that I was buying into her "wisdom".

One time, the co-founder of this particular group said to me, "Bev, there are two things that get people drinking again. One, is their ego. The other, is self-pity." So, I attempted to listen and pray more for the willingness, to do what I must do.

I was loving recovery, the people and the program. I didn't always love what people had to say to me, about me, though. Despite any criticism or wise advice, I was still feeling grateful to be where I am and I told everyone that would listen to me. I would be talking to my family about my new life and you could always see the shades go down over the eyes. They knew less what to say about all this "spiritual recovery" talk, than they did with my behavior before arriving here. Most didn't understand what was deep under the surface and simply were glad I wasn't drinking and behaving, the way I was. I would gab on and on about this new program, and they'd look at me like I was crazy, and I suppose I still was.

Shortly after that first meeting, Dave said to me "you are a changed person."

I felt that too.

Three weeks later, after my last drink, I came home from one of these gatherings. My home, that used for feel so cold, empty and dead to me, was now full of people and celebration. It was my birthday and they sang, we ate cake and had a grand time. My home was now a place of love and hope.

I could feel a big difference in myself but as well, other people were starting to recognize a change in me. Identifying the change or the changes to come, I couldn't articulate. What I did know is, that in my past when people would talk to me, they would wonder why such a nice person would behave in such a way. Whether it was the doctors, family or friends, they would talk about me and what I should be doing differently and I would feel such shame. Despite anyone's kindness they were attempting to direct towards me, I always felt worse, not better. I knew they did not have a clue of how I felt and it just felt condescending. The difference now is, I would hear peoples share their stories of the trials, tribulations and pains that they lived through, with their alcoholism, and I could identify with them. It made sense to me and there was a connection to something deeper within me.

These people in this program had been drinking and now they no longer were. But this recovery wasn't just about quitting drinking. It was a spiritual program of recovery. Prior to landing in this group, all we did was talk about the drinking. Everyone couldn't stop discussing how much or the way I drank. But this program, the drinking was only one part, a crucial part but just the first part of recovery. The big work was to come, after we stopped consuming alcohol.

The head psychiatrist at the London Psychiatric Hospital once told me, "There is nothing wrong with you having a few cold beers on a warm summer evening...just pace yourself." That psychiatrist once walked me down to another floor of the hospital and showed me other patients on the Korsakoff wing. A wing for patients with "wet brain" -a type of irreversible brain damage that can occur after extended and repeated exposure to heavy drinking. She would tell me; I would end up like them if I didn't pace myself. Everyone talked about the drinking but no one talked about the underlying problems. The fact was that most folks didn't know what alcoholism even was, including the doctors and now I know there is a stark difference between heavy drinking and suffering from the disease of alcoholism.

This program I was now in, was designed by people that knew. They knew alcoholics were powerless over alcohol and needed to quit drinking altogether and to heal their soul sickness, through this spiritual program. At the meetings, they would talk about mental obsession and physical allergy, and alcoholism being the spiritual disease of "more". I had never heard this before. No one ever told me I needed to stay away from that first drink. I remembered the lady in the psychiatric ward telling me her husband had a drinking problem and one was too many, and a thousand was never enough.

I could relate to it all now.

Now, I had the awareness that alcohol was what I used to cope and became my addiction, while I became sicker and sicker but it was not the root cause. I tried filling the hole in my soul with affection from men, attention from others, or drinking away this feeling of living in opposition to the way my soul knew I should be. The grace of something much bigger than me, found me awakening and insightful to this awareness.

Through the teachings, I was discovering that as humans we are all powerless to some degree because there is a power greater than ourselves. If we had all the power, we would have control of our lives and we wouldn't be in the despair of where we are or blaming the world for our predicaments. I slowly was learning that the real empowerment came from within me and through my greater power, God. I was sick enough and had just enough scrap of humility, to listen to the people in my spiritual program as I knew is that I had become powerlessness. So, I would surrender and hand it over to a power stronger than myself, as they told me to.

The gradual procession of willingness to follow this spiritual program, kept me going. I knew I wanted to keep trying. The gifts I was given, was that Dave got me to this program and I possessed the agreeability to listen to what was suggested to me and had the ability and willingness to continue listening to them, whether I knew what they were talking about or agreed with what they were saying, or not. I am strong willed person, and I had my own ideas for sure in my head, but I did what I was told to do, to succeed. I knew there was much to learn on most days.

By the summer time of 1971, I was excited about being where I was at. People were telling me they couldn't believe the change in me and complimenting me how good I was looking. This was slightly disconcerting to me as I often believed that I used always look good. After all, I was not a daily drinker but a binge drinker and it wasn't uncommon to be around others when I wasn't drinking. When I did binge, after a few days of recovery, I would get my hair done, do myself up nice and make the appearances of being well, despite the inside of me being broken. I would march around in a nice outfit like I was just fine, even though I wasn't. Now, the compliments hit differently. Now, I looked good and I felt good.

My mentor taught me to pray and ask for help every morning and to be a lady, and say thank you. To give gratitude each day for all that I had. I was obedient, and I got down on my knees each morning to ask for help and give thanks each evening. Some members of our group, had a hard time with some of these principles. I did not. It came naturally, for whatever reason.

I was feeling hopeful. I became preoccupied with how good I felt and the changes that were occurring in my life. I was being supportive of new folks coming to the recovery group and I was attempting to be the mother to David, that he deserved.

That June, another parent-teacher conference occurred. The first, since the February meeting. The first, since I got help. The teacher couldn't believe what a change there was in David. She said they had never seen such a change in a student's behavior as they did in David, in such a short period of a few months. The fact was there was now consistency and rules. When I was still drinking, there was no discipline or I would be feeling guilty for the ways I was acting, so I would make all kinds of compensation and allowances for everything he would do. Or if I did lay down some rules there was zero consistency, because by the time I got implementing them, I would binge again. The only thing that was ever persistent then, was that I felt guilty, all of the time. Now, there was dependability and it was encouragement for me to keep doing what I was doing.

That fall, there was a large conference with folks attending from all over that were in recovery, that I attended. At one point, I was asked to get up and say a few words, as one of the "newbies" at the podium in front of the large crowd. As I've said, it has never bothered me to do these sorts of things and I am well spoken, so I did. I shared that the longer I was sober and the longer I was in this program of spiritual healing, the more I understood about my own spiritual disease.

When I got done off the stage from speaking, the man that had started the conference years prior, approached me. He was impressed by what I shared and asked me for my contact information, as he wanted me to be a guest speaker at this same conference, in one year.

I received quite a bit of praise from others, often from men as they were the majority in this recovery group at this time. My mentor Geri would keep me in check. She was very protective of the ample praise I was recipient of, knowing that too much flattery, was not good for me. She knew enough, that although I was crazy and had done shameful things, I no less, had an ego. She had seen this before. Someone like me, grabbing the recovery reigns with both hands and doing well, and all the praise ended up being detrimental to their recovery. She was concerned that all flattery would go to my head and that I would take credit for the recovery I was experiencing, rather than giving the credit to where it belonged. I had to be reminded, that without this spiritual recovery program, without handing it all over to God in my powerlessness, that none of this would be happening. Never mind what I was doing, it was not an "I" program but a "we" and that without the people that had come before me here, that were willing to share their stories and experiences with me, *that*, gave me hope to stay and continue on.

Later at this conference, I was sitting in the audience, listening to the spiritual panel, the same panel I was just asked to speak at in one year. I was feeling divinely touched as I reflected on the fact that just a few months before I was destitute with unliveable pain, remorse and shame for the indecent, double-life I was living and now, *now*, the suffering was lifted and I was glowing, thanks to this recovery program.

A woman named Henriette, from Buffalo was sitting on one side of me and Garnett, a man from Detroit was sitting on the other side of me. A woman with many years of recovery, that they called Mickey, was the guest speaker on this spiritual panel. As she stood on the stage, she spoke about her children and how she had not been able to take care of them properly before she found healing. Obviously, I could identify.

As I listened and soaked up her knowledge and experience, I remember starring at her and thinking I saw a light or energy above her head, almost like it was a halo. Then, there was a transcendent energy, behind us in the auditorium, that I could feel. It was palpable and powerful. It was as though a higher power, or God, or something, was radiating from the back, with arms engulfing and embracing, Mickey, Garnett, Henriette, me and us all. From the back of this auditorium, this large room was immersed and we were all being held in this divine presence and I could feel it clearly.

In that moment, a true sense and feeling of belonging overcame me. I didn't know exactly what I belonged to but I felt a deep connection on a profound level. I just knew we were in this together and that I am home with these folks and this program.

I continued to read everything that was in sight about spirituality and any literature that was produced and I began to identify with others. I was calling people, talking to people, and submerging myself with spiritual recovery. I would support people at the weekly gatherings and shared what was given to me so freely when I arrived here. Each morning, I would ask for help and every evening, give thanks. When I was doing for others, I automatically felt better. I learned that when I did feel low or discouraged, if I went and found someone else to assist, I always felt heightened, through the identification of one soul-sick person, to another. These spiritual tools continued to allow me to feel uplifted.

In my discovery and reading of literature in the field of addiction, I came to understand that most success came from following certain spiritual steps.   I read about some of the founders of this spiritually healing program that included many doctors, psychiatrists, other alcoholics, priests, and spiritual leaders. They came to understand that helping other afflicted men and woman to identify a seemingly hopeless state of mind and body, through identifying with one and another through discussion and to show precisely how others have recovered through a spiritually based plan, worked. After all, it is a spiritual disease.

There was an understanding that spirituality was a key component. That it wasn't simply about quitting this or that, or getting therapy, but a healing of your soul, as well. They understood it was not religious but spiritual, and affliction to men and women of all walks of life, was present. Therefore, they understood to use a non-denominational, non-religious understanding and that God was a God of your choice or a power greater than us, which for some, was simply the people that have stayed sober and started to heal and the need to listen to them.

The complex layers of the plan were plenty but at the same time it was just as simple as that; stop drinking, follow the plan and heal. I was taught to get honest, really honest. Many people under the spell of spiritual disease, think that "it's not that bad" or "I will just slow down and control it." I knew, that simply wasn't the truth. The feeling of having shared a common peril with another is a binding, necessary and a powerful cement. We may have different details to our past stories or have different problems, but now have found common solutions to our ailing, suffering spirits. Words can not express how important and powerful it is to talk, and to listen to others that I could identify with.

I also needed the courage to be honest and to face the truth of my past and my actions. Some of this was very painful. But these new people I met taught me to live with courage so that I can have a fresh start, without forgetting my past completely. So, I practiced integrity by talking through all the shame and guilt that resided within me and about all my mistakes. I took inventory of my past and made lists and lists and lists.

I found hope finally. I had always had a higher power, from a young age. Now, a greater understanding, that I should never give up that faith, even when I suffered any sort of setback or challenge. Perhaps, especially then. I continued to pray daily to keep that hope and faith alive, to restore my mind and my sanity. I put my trust at the mercy of my higher power, over the selfishness and self-centredness of my affliction. I knew that at the base of it, my afflicted personality will always be at the bottom of it all, despite the healing happening now. Through this, I developed a greater trust, in my understanding of God.

This didn't mean that everything straightened out and I was level as a pool table now. It just meant that I was making changes and being provided tools that would allow me to live, in a way that I thought I should be living in the first place. I understood that this was not an event, it is a process. My family soon learned too, that they were not to book me for anything on a Tuesday, as each week I would return to this gathering of like-minded souls, to continue to heal and be there for others. I have met some great friends in my Tuesday group. Alex, a fellow that got sober three days before me, was good a friend and we would go to the meetings together. I got to be friends with his wife too and both of them with Dave. Alex and I would often joke that it was like the titanic and we were just hanging on to the people that were surviving, to stay alive.

I was developing a deep recognition that I had to forgive myself for my short comings but as well, accept others for theirs. A wise member of my group told me, that if I expect other people to accept me with my short-comings, then I better accept other people for theirs. That holds me in good stead, as ultimately there is not a human being on the face of the earth that does not have short comings. Some are easier to get along with than others but we all have them. If I want to think that other people are accepting me, warts and all, then I better accept other people too.

While I wasn't sure how much I had changed, I would gain insight to the changes through the observations, words and actions of others. Dave, who had been averse to going on his annual fishing trip for years, for fear of what would happen to me or David, decided to go this year. He didn't have a worry in the world and he went fishing.

He knew I had changed.

It's been one year since my last drink and finding recovery and a spiritual way of living. While the folks in this group understood, very few outside of it comprehended what alcoholism really was. Everyone understands the damage done by drinking, the stupid and immoral things we had done and how awful we behaved. It caused distress for everyone it touched, thus, why they often referred to it as a family disease. That is what my family, usually focused on and they're not wrong.

However, I am learning this has very little to do with what is wrong with us. It wasn't about the wine I was drinking; it was the shame, guilt, remorse and soul sickness that created spiritual bankruptcy within me. While the quitting of alcohol was imperative, living in recovery was to heal and live a spiritual life.

I also understood that not everyone got sick the same way. For some, the first time they drank, it was the answer and relief they were looking for in challenges. Others blacked out after their initial experience. I was not that way.

When I had my first drink when I was 19. I was attending my staff Christmas party at our manager's place. The home was beautiful, the fire place was roaring, the Christmas tree sparkling and everyone was dressed to the nines. All the big wigs were there. They were serving fancy beverages in long stem flutes, off of silver trays. I only had a couple drinks and I had the absolute best time. As far as I was concerned, I had arrived in life.

While I continued to drink after that night and I could drink a fair amount, I did not drink alcoholically and I was still behaving in an appropriate way, for many years. I have a deeper understanding with each day in recovery, that as my soul became sicker, I began to drink more, in order to feel better, to feel more comfortable. There was something within me that was thirsty for a higher purpose of living, but I couldn't articulate what it was, I just knew I went unquenched. I quite simply couldn't stand the person, I had become.

    I had been looking to live a spiritual way, my whole life. Finding it again now, through the Grace of God and through the people of this program, allowed me to be living a happier and healthier life, one year later. I had re-found my spiritual way of living and the hole within my soul, slowly was beginning to fill.

    It was custom to commemorate this new way of life with an annual celebration. Celebrating of the individual, while offering hope to those that are new. Now, it was my turn, my one-year celebration. They liked to call it a birthday, as it is anniversary of the day my life was given new breath. It was the anniversary of my spiritual re-birth.

I wasn't sure what all the fuss for my annual celebration was about. I often thought that everyone that came into recovery had the same process and evolutional process through this new spiritual living, as I did. I didn't survey or ask folks how they were rating their progress or anything, but I just assumed we all felt similarly. I could tell however, by the response of others towards myself, that many had not seen a recovery so pronounced or witness someone change in such a short period of time.

Recovery folks saw that I was in this, with a full-tilt enthusiasm and they would tell me so. I was being asked to speak to other groups all over the place outside of the city. I would speak from my soul, and not my head. This was recognized by others and I received much praise for it, much to the chagrin of my mentor Geri and others, who often would worry about my ego getting in the way of my continued success. Perhaps, they had grounds for their fret and I am not discounting that. I did know however, there was a spiritual awakening within me. I was happy, I was living the way I knew I should be living; I was being the mother I should be to David and my relationship with Rick and Cathy, was improving. Glimpses of good things happening, along with feelings of my spiritual thirst being satisfied, felt good.

So, on this evening, of my one-year celebration mark, we gathered. The place was packed. When I got up in front of everyone, I looked out at all the people, and there was my Dave, he looked so proud. He and many others, looked back at me while I spoke, with smiles and pleasant looks. The energy of the room was lovely. I sensed and felt these people really cared for me and were happy for my life. My heart was full and I felt so richly blessed and grateful.

While I was committed to nurturing this moment, I couldn't help but think that had this been my regular birthday, all my family would have been here, but they were not. Dave was and that was enough. I was not complaining but pondering. The only other person that ever went to a spiritual meeting with me was my sister's husband Jim, my brother-in-law. Jim and my Aunt Mary seemed to understand that this was all more than the chaos caused by my behaviors and that there was a deeper sickness to be healed, and they supported that. The rest of the family wasn't thinking, "oh good, Bev is now on a spiritual path" but rather they were just glad I wasn't drinking anymore and that I was taking care of David, as I ought to be. They didn't understand that drinking was only a symptom of my suffering soul. It could have been anything to numb the reality, as it is for so many. My story, simply involved alcoholism as the "ism" of my dis-ease.

But, if the psychiatrists didn't know the ins and outs of this disease, how on earth could I expect my family to understand it?

Either way, ponderings aside, I felt richly blessed.

Two days after this celebration, my father took myself, my brother Donnie and my daughter Cathy, now 16 years old, to Florida. We had a lovely time, despite Cathy having a broken leg.

Life was simply different now, better. The shame-latent guilt and the painful suffering was lifting, layer by layer. I was fully submerged in this new way of living. I was eternally grateful to be feeling the way I was and not living the life I had.

That summer, I was in the garden in the backyard at my home. I loved to be in the elements and with my hands in the dirt. I was on my knees, digging, planting and pulling weeds by the back steps, and then it happened again. The divine presence I felt that day, in the auditorium last fall. I had this profound feeling of rays of light shining on and surrounding me. I could feel God's presence. I felt a warmth, a love and a knowing that I was safe, and being looked after, and I knew I was on the right track.

I was reminded of a hymn that I had learned when I was younger. "I have come to the garden alone, while the dew was still on the roses, and He talked with me and he walked with me, and He told me, I, am his own."

It was a short lived, but undeniable experience.

It was fall of 1972. A man, I now knew as Jamie, had asked me to speak on a spiritual panel at a conference in Guelph the year before. Most of the people on this panel were seasoned veterans with 25 plus years of spiritual recovery. While I didn't fully understand why I was asked to speak, I did understand that I must be doing something right and that I was a good speaker. I often thought that many had died not finding this recovery, perhaps this was God's way, since I didn't die, of getting my attention and to serve some sort of higher purpose. Thus, I was pleased to be at this conference speaking, despite my naivete and newness.

My whole life I was good at getting up in front of others and speaking. This was different. I felt like a basket case and so, I prayed for strength. Nervously sitting in the crowd, awaiting my turn to talk about faith and spirituality, there was another gentleman beside me, who was also going to be speaking. He jokingly said "supposedly, we are getting up there to talk about faith, but here we are, sitting down here absolutely paralyzed with fear." The comedic relief of laughing at ourselves was welcomed.

I don't remember what I said much other than how I completely believed that I had turned my life over to God and that my life would restore. Others shared that what I said was good and that I did well. A priest by the name of Father Pete approached me and said, "If there was anybody here that heard you speak, that hadn't come to believe, then they just weren't listening."   I don't think I fully appreciated what he was expressing, and simply thanked him for his kindness.

I couldn't distinguish, as I was so fresh in this new life, but I glimpsed the meanings of what others were saying to me in regards to my healing. I was feeling like I was acting in a way that I could be proud of and that my higher power would want of me. Although, I was not fully coherent to the extent of the healing done and the healing still to be had, I knew inside my soul, I had surrendered.

I have been reading one of my spiritual recovery books, bringing me to a greater understanding that I have handed my life over to something bigger than me and perhaps now, a servant of God or a higher power since coming into this new life, as countless others have before me. I was a sitting duck and take no credit for any of it. I felt this from the beginning, but not all did. Some have flashes of awakening. I didn't have a big flash but certainly had glimpses of my spiritual awakening. I don't think I could understand wholly but it appeared to other people I was emerged and surrendered. I do know that I was relieved of the obsession to drink, immediately once arriving to a spiritual recovery program.

Did I think about drinking? Sure. Any dinner party we were went to they were serving drinks. We recently went to a party at the Shanfield's with a Hawaiian theme and they were serving these beautiful alcoholic pineapple cocktails. Of course, you could hardly be sitting at these events and not think about drinking. It was not difficult for me to not drink; it was just different for me but not difficult, to abstain.

I had a strong desire to do whatever it was I needed to do, to not be sick again. I thought everyone had this desire and relief and ease with recovery but that is not the case. There were lots of people in this program that did not succeed or like being told what to do or how to live. Many thought they were better than this program, or smarter. I did not. The first few steps were delivered to me and received with an open heart.

I can recall many years ago, my neighbor that was deemed "alcoholic", a successful business man with a big beautiful home showcasing a grand piano. They had to put the house up for sale and sell everything in it due to the situation they were in. When they put the sale add in the paper, they asked if they could use my phone number. They didn't want the gentleman to know so he wouldn't get the money from the sale because he was drinking alcoholically. I never thought much about it.

Everyone drank alcohol, it seemed. I recall throughout high school and the years beyond, many saying how they loved to drink and how good it made them feel. They would talk about how much fun life was when drinking and how it helped them feel more social and like they belonged. I never felt that. I already felt confident and that life was good, or so I felt at the time. I never drank, until I did. I eventually refrained from refraining, as it was the thing to do at parties.

Many alcoholics talk about past trauma or mistreatment in their lives and it certainly is understandable and is the proof of justification for their soul sickness. I didn't have this same background. I think it is fair to say that I felt ease through my life for the most part, something many did not experience. I think it is also fair to say I wasn't the quiet wallflower that began drinking to feel more confident, I was probably considered one of the popular, outgoing gals growing up.

What I did have was the base recipe ingredients for spiritual dis-ease. I had some understanding of my past and the role it played in this sickness. I was starting to understand that blame had no place and the responsibility for my life was mine. I could no longer fault my problems on men that abandoned me or on World War 2. Understanding this dis-ease was not to excuse or condone the behavior from others that may have caused emotional, mental or physical abuse to these now adult-children when they were younger, but I understood that it is now solely the responsibility of each individual to heal the wounds of the past.

We all have a story. Each and everyone have a background that we could blame. However, there is no healing in blame or judgement. When we blame, we often villainize another or a situation and thus making ourselves the victim. Healing happens in responsibility of our own thoughts, feelings, actions and the way we live, right now!

We must investigate and take inventory of where we are and how we are in this moment. I was receptive to the fact that my mother was not an aware and affectionate mother but I had so many others that gave me that affection and love.

My father, I put all my eggs in his basket, he was my everything.

Recognizing that it is now up to me is where the power is. What I am going to do with my character flaws? No matter how we developed our spiritual dis-ease and flaws, no matter how terrible our childhood was, no matter how poorly we may have been treated, and certainly the scars that were produced from these experiences are justified and not to me minimized or invalidated, but continuing to stay in the pain of this, will not heal us.

I didn't have the awful story that many had to contend with, but that didn't mean I wasn't as crazy or sick as them. It perhaps blessed me to internalize this spiritual program with more ease and less need for outside healing. Many would say, if you had lived my life, you wouldn't find it so easy. Perhaps that is true. But we all need to peel away the layers because really, who comes through life without a scar?

The spiritual program was an answer. In order to get well, instead of relying on things on the outside world to make me feel good on the inside, I must rely on myself. I must go within. I know the ongoing need is to go inward and connect with my higher power.

I had the clarity that I needed to clear the wreckage of the past, of my past. It was clear and easy for me to recognize that the ways I needed to change, as this spiritual program presented clarity in a way that I could bare. The program also provided guidance and the confirmation of my ability to handle the changes that I need to make. As my awareness progressed and the layers were peeled back, I knew I needed to shed the shame and guilt for not living the way I should have lived in my past. I was learning how to live in this moment. I was be taught to go slow, peeling one layer at time. Otherwise, certainly if I had been made aware of all my wrong doings and flaws at once, I would have most certainly felt hopeless and ready to shoot myself. But God presented to me just what I could bare, in a way and at a rate that I could handle it. I made the changes that I became aware of as they came along. The very fact that I wasn't drinking and that I was now being a reliable and good person that I could look at in the mirror now, provided a clear understanding, that I was on the right track.

I could also see that sobriety and living a spiritual life were different. Many were staying sober but do not appear they have connected with their soul to do the spiritual healing. What comes from the heart, reaches the heart.

Historically, I had been looking for one more man, or external experience that would not and could not fill the hole in my soul. I knew I had to do the work and it needed to come from within myself. So many focus on the alcohol or the drugs, or the gambling, the excessive shopping, the sex, the trying to control others or whatever the external fixation was, to fill the hole. Certainly, my family had not been talking about the hole in my soul but how much I drank.

But of course, they didn't. I didn't understand it to be a spiritual disease until I arrived that day, so how would they?

I knew it was necessary and I wanted to understand my past and what led up to my spiritual death, but also it was necessary to investigate and focus on my behaviors and the damage it caused.

What is the need within ourselves that we are trying to achieve? Why do we gravitate to it and how and why do we stay focusing on the external situation? We have to eventually ask within ourselves, to heal ourselves, why we were gravitating towards the external experience?

The focus on ourselves is imperative. Always, always, always the focus is on the inside; how we are thinking, feeling and acting.   Never mind how someone else is behaving, we must focus on ourselves and what we need to do with our own actions. When we focus on the external situation, we lose ourselves and the potential to heal. This is the only way to achieve empowerment and healing.

I notice in this spiritual program that the more experienced folks that are doing it and getting it right, don't allow others to stay caught up in the repetitive (and sometimes obsessive) stories of the past. They will listen to others past-stories one time, allowing expression of the wrong-doings and the problems of their past, only to validate, legitimize and hear them, but they move the conversation in the direction of solution. *What changes do you need to make happen now? What is it about you that has to change? What is it about you that is allowing this to continue?*

Many will want to tell their awful stories over and over with different details or players in the story, but then we have to ask ourselves what it is in our soul that needs to heal? When we focus on the external details, we are keeping ourselves from going within, where the power is.

Those with a spiritual thirst tend to search to fill that hole and quench that thirst with a temporary reassuring external device of whatever kind, until they find true healing.

The fellowship of this spiritual recovery group assisted me to acknowledge an inner knowing that I was not the person I knew I wanted to be, that I could be and who I should be. Therefore, I didn't oppose anything suggested to me as I understood, my life had been unmanageable. I was grateful to be where I am now but knew I had so much further to journey.

I had been in recovery for about three years now. I was doing well or so I was feeling. All of the sudden, I had the answers for everyone, I was sponsoring and supporting any woman that asked me too and was speaking all over the place. The gals were having a big party for me at some fancy restaurant and got me a big bouquet of roses and so on. Now instead of being humble and grateful, I was thinking I was some big shot telling everyone else how to live. My mentor was not happy with them or me and this was difficult for her to watch. Properly concerned, she didn't want all the praise and accolades to allow my ego to take over my spirit. It was told to me the two most dangerous things for continued recovery were self-pity and ego and there was absolutely a danger that my ego would get the best of me. Reminding me, as these other people were looking up to me, that the only looking up to we should all be doing is to our higher power or the God of our understanding. Luckily, whatever Geri told me to do, I did, as my ego could be as big as a house otherwise.

So, I continued to pray for willingness to do what I needed to do. I trusted Geri, my mentor. I continued to give credit for whatever assistance and help I gave to others through speaking or support, to my higher power. Whether I felt humility or not, I understood I could get egotistical with an inferiority complex.

There were a handful of people that thought "who the hell does she think she is?" and I was curious why, as I thought I was friendly and I always brought sandwiches to the gatherings. They knew, my ego was rearing its head and knew putting me on a pedestal was dangerous to my ongoing health, healing and sobriety.

I observe that many can stay sober but they were not able to or it did not appear to me that they knew how to connect with the soul to do spiritual healing. I knew that there was a hole in my soul that not one more drink or one more man or whatever the external experience was, would fill that space. I knew what comes from the heart, reaches the heart. It could be shopping, sex, gambling, an abusive partner or even work. When any of these external situations are out of hand and we were unsuccessfully attempting to control and manipulate, we need to ask, why? Why is there this deep hole in the soul?

We have to eventually (to heal) ask within, why we gravitate to the certain external, for relief. What is the need within and why? How and why do we stay focused on the external situation?

Focusing on myself, after sharing with my fellow recovery people and telling them all the problems of my past, I now needed to turn to solution. What changes do I need to happen? What is it about me that has to change? Never mind what he did or she said and how you want them to change...what do *I* need to do to change and feel better? What is it in my soul that needs to heal?

I am now cognisant that those such as myself, that possess both, a spiritual thirst and feel the hole in their soul seek to quench the thirst and fill the hole with external sources as a quick remedy of temporary relief. I knew I needed to go within and above, to find new internal connection and resources to infuse the empty space within my spirit.

I started praying every morning to relieve the bondage of myself and this assisted me to not take any receiving of credit I didn't deserve, remembering where the power came from and I am not it. I needed to remember that.

I was fortunate to be presented and introduced to a spiritual program and provide healing to my soul. I feel this healing slowly day by day, by day. The sobriety and withdrawal management of the body was imperative so I can stay long enough to hear about the true healing and recovery of the spirit. I could now recognize that the longer I drank and the less I thought of myself, the sicker my soul got. It is not just about getting rid of the external addiction. I didn't drink because I was thirsty.   Now, the healing was moving into the mind, heart and soul.

  I was reining it in or rather it was a full-time job of my mentor to keep me reined in. She was tough on me. Fortunately, she was far more interested in getting me well rather than me liking her.   I acquired a little more humility now that I wasn't the big shot, I and others thought I was. Often when we get a little better, then we begin to give ourselves credit, instead of remaining humble and giving the credit to higher power. I often had a hard time understanding why she would say the things she said to me but I also understood that she has more recover and spiritual healing than me. She assisted me to find humility time and time again, and to continue to be able to serve with the gifts that I had been given.

  I was opinionated. Probably, always will be. I am not a wishy-washy human being. I am monitoring my strong opinionated ways and I am learning to listen to other people's opinions and be open to them whether I agree with them or not. I am learning they are entitled to their opinions, as I am to mine. I have more consciousness of when telling someone my opinion and they are not buying it. In the past, I would move closer and closer to them until I was trying to cram my opinion down their throats with my fists. I needed to honor that not everyone thought the same way as me. I began to listen to learn and learn by listening. This awareness was present, now I needed to begin to learn to practice this in my every day life.

I knew this was an opportunity and the next layer, for more growth and healing.

To clear the wreckage of my past, I had started the practice of taking a fearless moral inventory of myself, each and every year, on the anniversary of my recovery and sobriety. Initially, I was hyper-focused and concentrating on the affects of my life on my children and my lustful ways, and I didn't look much further. I simply felt that if I stopped behaving in those ways, I would be fine and I think my husband felt the same.

This is where I needed to start but there was much more work to be done.

I decided to examine annually, my position with the seven deadly sins; envy, gluttony, greed, lust, pride/vanity, sloth and wrath. As I said, initially I just felt the ways I behaved as an unresponsible wife was the main issue. I had so much loathing for what I had done, that I believed I didn't have issue with pride, but I did. I had a lot of false-pride. I wanted things so different in my life and in my past and didn't want anyone to know the truth of who I had become, but had to accept myself where I was in life and who I am. I would lie, cheat or steal to prevent anyone from knowing the truth of my reality. I need to face this now.

Although I was still whipping myself for all my wrong-doings and replaying the terrible saga of my past, I was also following this spiritual recovery program and it was bringing me more peace, more healing and more ease.

I also, had been blaming myself for experiences that were not my fault at all. I was just taking responsibility for everything. Slowly, sifting through the piles of time, I looked at the seven deadly sins, figuring out what was mine to own and what was not. I knew I (like all of us) had a bit of every sin within and I needed to examine this.

The least impactful for whatever reason, for me, was envy. I rarely was a jealous person.

You couldn't have convinced me that I suffered from sloth, as I was always doing something. However, I am now more enlightened to the fact that I was doing what I wanted to do, when I wanted to do it, so it would demonstrate to everybody how busy-busy I was and blah-blah-blah, but I wasn't doing some of the things I should have been doing, like cleaning my house, as an example. I was able to see that I neglected some things that needed to be done and that was my sloth inventory.

I associated anger with people throwing things and fighting, screaming and yelling and I didn't do any of that. As a result, I had repressed all my anger for the ways that I had been treated or the unfair events in my life, but I was only becoming aware of this through glimpses.

I would write pages and pages of my wrong-doings, especially of lust. It was also important that I not only admit these wrong-doings to myself and to the God of my understanding but to share this with another human being. There is a power of sharing and saying things out loud.

Last year, I had read my novel of written wrong doings to a priest. I can still see his face. He must have been so damn bored, as I read pages and pages, as he was practically falling asleep. I can still remember where we were sitting, what he was wearing and all the details. The words he spoke are unforgettable to me to this day.   "Bev, your higher power has forgiven you. It would behove you to forgive yourself."

So, I continued to try.

Each year, I go within, for a deep dive inventory of myself and my life. Each year, I learn and expand and gain a better understanding of myself. I also, continue to pray and meditate to be ready and remove my shortcomings.

This was not a fast forward process but a gradual healing, in stages. I was learning to live a spiritual life, slowly but surely.

Chapter 6

The mid-1970s

I have been living a spiritual life for about four to five years now. I was asked to be Chairwoman of the Western Conference for spiritual recovery.

Looking back, I now realize that I didn't know diddley squat the first years of my recovery, despite thinking I knew everything. I thought everyone should be listening to me and if they did, they'd be happier like me. That was arrogance. When Geri would put me in my place, instead of reacting, I was starting to understand the necessity. She was quiet and steady. I was loud and up and down and flamboyant. I had confused her personality, thinking her to be quiet and peaceful, rather than just an individual working quietly on her own spiritual practice while not feeling the need to put her two cents into everything. This seemed foreign to me.

Each year as I grew, I knew it was less about how I appeared to others but what healing was happening in my soul. Never mind, blaming and minimizing my life on anyone, I was owning my life.

Over the last couple of years, the physical and mental healing had happened and now, emotional leveling was occurring through the constant shift of ongoing personal inventory, daily and in more depth, each year.

We don't know, what we don't' know. *As long as we do a little better today than we did yesterday, that will continue to be my goal.* I don't judge where I am today, but simply commit to understand that its not good or bad but just different. Each stage, each layer, each year, I grow and shift and the hole in my soul becomes less gaping.

I can now examine my past and see how far I have come. When I feel the guilt and shame of living a life in contradiction to how I know I should have been living, I can comprehend the layers that have healed. I no longer had to lie or cheat. I no longer hide in bathrooms in shame. I no longer drink alcohol. I continue to dismantle the cloaks of my yesterdays, while staying present in the moment, living one day at a time.

My spiritual healing and recovery also came to see that my views and judgments (usually just of myself) needed to also include others. When you have been to hell and back you start to feel more compassion and empathy to those in hell or taking their first steps out of the flames. I actively became less judgemental of others and their stories and experiences. They were me; I was them, with different details.

As I gradually lean into myself more and more, I understood I still had triggers from my past. I prayed to be open, honest and willing to turn my defects over, to continue to keep my ego in check and to take inventory and responsibility for my thoughts, feelings and actions. Gratefully, I did all this by continuing to have a strong sponsor.

One day I said to Geri, "the longer I am in spiritual recovery and sobriety, the less I seem to know." In her quiet way, as only she could have produced, she said "that is the most intelligent thing I've heard you say." Five years into this healing process, I had just enough humility to take in her wisdom and understanding of her proclamation.

She continued to assist me to understand where my own healing as well as me sharing and helping others, could happen more effectively from a grounded place.

And boy, did I need to stay grounded.

The year is 1977. My father's health was compromised, and that spring, he moved in to our home. I liked taking care of him. It was easy for me to do. My sweet husband Dave was also very good at helping with of my dad. It fed my soul and felt right, that I was in a place in my life and in my recover that I was able to do this.

Unfortunately, as the spring sprung, my father's health was declining and he was dying. He had been admitted to University Hospital, where I would visit regularly. He was becoming less responsive day by day. I would hold his hand and let him know I was there and he would blink. He knew I was present.

I had been praying for my dad's health for weeks. My friend, who was a minister would tell me, "Bev, you not only are trying to arrange things here on earth, but you are trying to arrange things in heaven too".

I just simply wanted God to know what a fine man my dad had been and was. No matter what his short comings were, he was an honest, good man.

One morning, on my way to work at the Latin Quarter Restaurant, I decided to go the St. Peter's Basilica church. It was a large and beautiful church downtown London, Ontario. I got down on my knees to pray at the alter. The place was quiet, dark and I was alone with my higher power, with my head bowed.

Then something divine happened.

The church lit up. A bright and brilliant light all of the sudden beamed so brightly down from the steeple and on to the alter. The sun was not shining. It was wild, to say the least. A moment later, up in the balcony, the organ began to play music. Being alone in the church, I was in awe and felt the presence of God's grace, comforting me in this moment.

I recognized this to be one of those moments of connection with my higher power. In the past, when I had shared to Sister St. Patrick, my experiences like this, such as at the conference or in the garden and she would often say, "you talk about these experiences like everyone has them. They don't. You should be grateful and amazed that you have had as many spiritual, ethereal and celestial encounters, as you have." I was.

I eventually got up off my knees and made my way to work. When I walked in, John, my boss, told me that University Hospital had called and wanted me to call them back. I said to him "I am sure my father has passed away." He said, "oh Bevvy, I am sure they just called to talk to you and give you a status report."

I called the hospital to get an update. Exactly at the moment, when the light, lit up the dark and the quiet church and the organ played music, my father had died.

I felt that my higher power was with me in that moment and answered me.

I heard you. He was a good man. He is with me in heaven now.

My connection with David grew stronger and we have developed a deeper, loving bond. I was involved in Rick and Cathy's lives more too. They were older now and making choices on their own and with less influence from their father. They both were married now and I was grateful to be a part of that.

Cathy often came to visit me which I was so happy about. Rick was up to his eye balls playing sports, so I would go and watch, any time I could. I didn't get to spend a lot of time with him as he was busy with the activity or sport of the day, but now his wife, Brenda, included me in all the family events which I was simply so appreciative of.

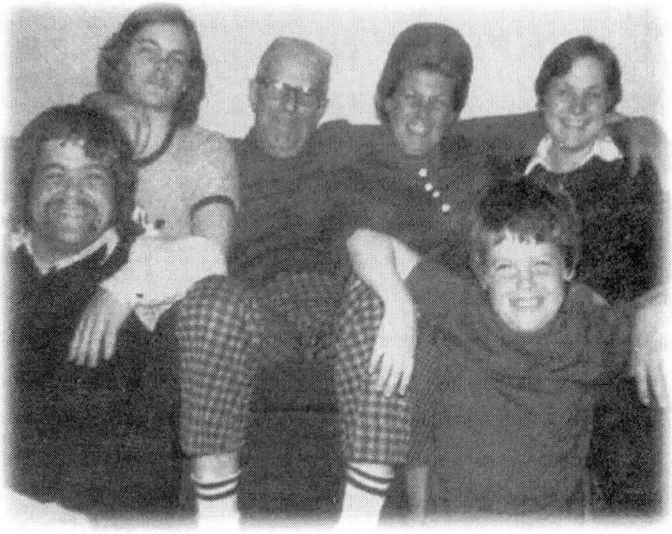

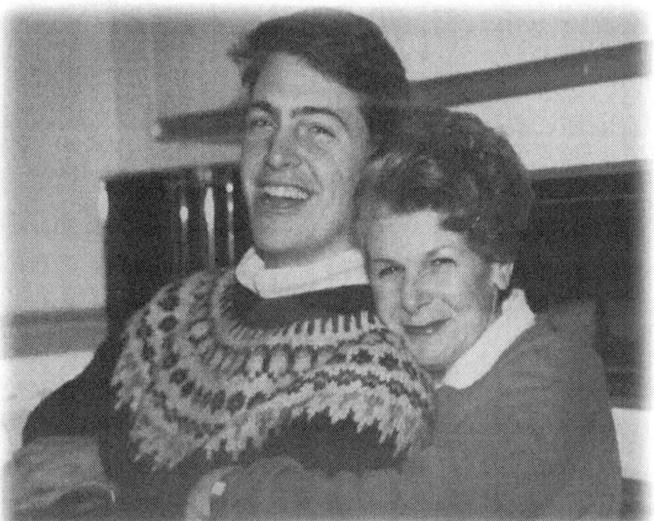

Chapter 7

The 1980s

My mentor, my friend and my inspiration, Geri, was a heavy smoker. I had been in recovery for 10 years under her wing, when she was diagnosed with lung cancer. My boss, John Downs, would let me do what I felt like doing for the most part, and this allowed me to take Geri to her appointments, tests and procedures. Geri's daughter, Meredith had become part of my close circle too. Meredith was a University Professor in Northern Ontario and I would keep her updated with medical happenings with her mother.

As Geri's disease progressed, Meredith came home to London to spend more time with her mother. We all certainly knew she was very ill. I had a friend that was a nurse that worked on the same floor that Geri was admitted to, so we received thorough updates.

My son David, now 17 years old, became good pals with Meredith. David would take Meredith dinners up to the hospital floor, on Sunday nights. We had her stay with us often and we all spent a lot of time with her during this period, while Geri was hospitalized.

On one particular Tuesday, I went up in the afternoon to visit this woman who had changed and shaped my life. I talked to her that day and told her how grateful I was for her and everything she had done for me and what she meant to me and my life. I told her how grateful I was that Al introduced me to her or maybe talked her into being my sponsor and mentor. I knew her disease was bad and wanted to make sure I expressed this to her. I felt peaceful.

Tuesday recovery meeting was still very much a part of my weekly routine. That same day, Bee, a good pal of mine, who was also mentored by Geri, and I headed to our meeting. Meredith and David headed up to see Geri.

That night, while we were tucked away at our spiritual meeting, and in the presence of her daughter and my son, Geri passed away.

After the meeting when I got home, I found out. Bee and I, although saddened, often mused that Geri made sure we were out of her way, for her to transition.

Meredith asked me to do the eulogy at Geri's funeral and so I did.

It felt like a lovely tribute to me, as it did to many others. It was so sincere because I owed her so much and loved her so dearly.

The days after, I was moaning and groaning about the loss of my spiritual guide. My old friend, Davey Stone told me to get a new one. My mentor was gone and although I did not require the reining in that I once did, I did require someone to keep me honest and real. I asked Bee, who was a steady presence and influence in my life, to be my new mentor and sponsor.

Davey also told me it was time for me to step up. He would remind me to keep it simple but that it was time to fill the void of Geri, by rising to the occasion.

A couple years had passed, and I was doing whatever I could do to mentor others, keep myself grounded, and be aware of my own thoughts and behaviors.

I had a grandchild now. Rick and Brenda had a boy, Christopher.

Unfortunately, Rick was dealing with more than new fatherhood. My oldest son called me about difficulties he was having with his marriage and with his alcohol consumption. The problems had been festering within his marriage for sometime apparently and he drank alcohol problematically and seemingly out of his control.

The straw that broke camels back was when he went out drinking on a Saturday evening and didn't come home. That Sunday morning, he was to do something with his wife, for her grandmother. He was unable to, again. His wife told him that he may be okay with living life this way, but she and Christopher would not be continuing to do so.

That Monday morning, he called me to share that he quit drinking. I introduced him to my good friend Brian and he spent some time with him and some other fellows from our spiritual recovery program. He started going to weekly recovery meetings as well.

Rick was a deep thinker, deeper than one might think he appears to be. He wasn't an overly emotional creature, which may be why there was less damage done by his childhood, than perhaps his sibling. He quit, just like that. He had said he didn't want to end up to be the same type of father as his father had been.

Rick began to see the healing and the benefits of spiritual recovery. He would often share that he could see that his step-father Dave was good for him, and to me. He could see all the good that was going on in my life now.

There was a ripple effect.

I had a new sponsor. I had a new life. I decided a new business would be a fun decision. I started a part-time catering business with my neighbor and friend, Louise. I kept my job at Latin Quarter and the owner, John was very supportive of my decision in developing this gourmet catering biz. He allowed me to use equipment and storage and so on. It was feeling good. We were catering to all the big-wigs and events.

I was very busy, attempting to keep up with my job, my business, my family and my personal recovery. I had an understanding that my recovery, my spiritual recovery would be ongoing and there was no finish line.

There wasn't a second that I wasn't a busy-busy bee and I loved it, it fed my soul. I was feeding people and they loved our food. They say food feeds the soul. This was a win-win. I just adored it all.

My catering partner and I were leading this fast-paced life for about two years now when my friend Brian stopped by to have lunch with me. Brian also a part of my recovery program and assisting my son, was a good friend. While munching together, he threw out this idea that he had to open a treatment centre for people needing substance recovery. Now, at this point of my life, I am running in every direction at all times with my job, my business, my family and so on, but none the less, I say "I have often thought about doing something like that."

It was just a comment. I meant that would be a nice thing to do, but I hadn't really thought about actually working with alcoholics or addicts as a career, not to mention there wasn't anytime in my life to do such as thing.

The next day, the phone rang and it was Brian. He said "I have been thinking about your comment from yesterday, have you given it any more consideration?" I replied "anymore consideration about what?" He referenced my off-the-cuff comment about opening a treatment centre. I had not given it another thought after the words had spilled casually from my mouth. In fact, I had actually forgot about that part of the conversation. Not waiting for any further reply from me, Brian stated, "well, I have given it a lot of thought and I think you would be great for this".

Before long in this conversation, I told him I would think on it, as I wanted to chat with Dave about it as well as my dear friend, Sister St. Patrick. I honestly thought they would both say "don't be a fool", you like what you are doing.

They did not.

I asked Dave, he thought I might be good to do something like this. I called Sister St. Patrick and she said "I can't think of a reason why this wouldn't be a good idea for you."

I was fifty years old and I loved the catering business. My son David was away at university. It was fall, and we had events booked for the whole holiday season. However, my last catering event was New Years Eve 1983.

My partner in this catering business needed a collaborator and associate to run this business and my ultimate decision to leave this business in exchange for this new project was challenging and disappointing for both her and her husband.

I felt sad to leave the field of food and perhaps even more so, saddened by the problematic strain it created with my friends and business partners. I left my job at the Latin Quarter, as well.

In January of 1984, we began to slowly roll the wheels into motion. As with most big changes, there are strains and stresses. Grieving the loss of what was, while attempting to establish the new often presents a ruffling of feathers and a lack of comfort. In fact, the business of attempting to initiate a treatment and recovery centre was a very difficult and stressful time. There were some neigh-sayers and folks that were concerned, and others that were frankly very upset with my decision. Ultimately, my disturbed feelings strengthened by faith and belief in what we were doing. My motives and intentions, were pure.

Sister St. Patrick let me suffer. She never once told any of us to stop. Instead, she said "if you don't get some blood in your veins, you'll never last."

She allowed me to get stronger.

Up until this point I was pampered in my spiritual recovery. I had been accustomed to adulation, adoration and attention. So, the folks that said what I was doing, was wrong or I wasn't doing it right, propelled me further. I wrote many of the higher ups in the program to get direction and perhaps approval. I got it. They sent me binders, literature and any information I needed about opening a treatment centre. This recovery centre would not be associated with my spiritual program of recovery but it would be modelled after it with a body, mind and spirit approach.

While still, some men chattered disapprovals in the shadows, I soldiered on with Brian and the others. I knew these challenges, pushbacks and difficult opinions of others would ultimately strengthen my fortitude and determination. If I did not have the faith that I possessed or the strong belief that we were doing what was right, I would have crumbled in the unsupportive judgements from others, perhaps. Eventually, when we were given the approval and the support from the spiritual program for our separate venture, all but one of the cynics and detractors, offered an apology and their support. My faith grew stronger yet.

Sister St. Patrick was a stable support that kept me from being wishy-washy and assisted me to stand tall. She had connections too. I had meetings and dinners at the home of the President of the Addiction Research Foundation (ARF) because she/we knew somebody that knew somebody.   Dr. Brian Rush, a specialist affiliated with the Centre of Addiction and Mental Health took a liking to me and supported me anyway he could. He developed all sorts programs of recovery and gave us guidance.

My dear husband continued to support me. He got me a credit card and a car and I was on my way.

The next year and a bit, were shaky. There were many wheels already in motion. We had support and programs from top professionals in their field. What we didn't have, was the government funding yet.

The cart was before the horse.

Before I had signed on, Brian and some friends, had found an Inn called the Westover Inn, up in St. Mary's. They developed and incorporated the name, Westover Treatment Centre and the Westover Foundation. They were going to buy the Inn but ultimately it was too much money and the deal fell through. They had ordered all kinds of beautiful furniture to fill the rooms of a centre that wasn't even established yet.

They found another building which had been a nursing home, a big old Victorian home up in Thamesville, which the county had lost funding for the beds. It had sat there for a couple years for sale. A big house, a bungalow and an acre of land. They were offered the property very cheap, but again, they didn't have the money.

They had a potential property, they had a name registered but only had a little money coming from here and there, not enough to buy or complete the renovations to open a treatment centre.

When I came on board to this project, I initially was in charge of public relations and fundraising. There was a man named Art, that had signed on to run the treatment centre, and he rented himself an Oldsmobile and got Brian a Buick and Nancy a Chevrolet. Despite my job with this team requiring me to drive around, he didn't get me one, as he didn't like me much. I had disagreed with what and how they were doing things and told Art so. They were spending money that wasn't there and I thought it was crazy. Understandably, I challenged him and he didn't like me for it but I said what had to be said.

Gratefully, I had the car Dave bought me.

I would go to businesses where they had ordered all this furniture and supplies but couldn't pay for it. I always dragged Sister St. Patrick with me, dressed in her nun habit. I would explain what our treatment centre was about, I would tell them the truth about no funding yet, and that all the stuff the others had ordered, we simply afford and we couldn't take items ordered. Sister St. Patrick would then beg for their forgiveness and she would get it. We took the three rental cars back because we couldn't afford them. There was no money to pay for any of this stuff.

Again, the cart was before the horse.

By this time, businesses in Thamesville were sick and tired of us and we hadn't even opened yet.

I was bucking the current of the others but I knew the doors would be closed before they were opened, if I didn't do something.

I had called people at other treatment centres to get advice. Art didn't like that but I was okay with it. I didn't like he wasn't so keen on me but I felt good that I was strong enough to seek the help this sinking ship needed to keep afloat.

It was very challenging times. I got through it as I had lots of support. What I was saying and that I had the courage to tell the truth and not care about the optics of it was good. The others were worried sick about the honesty of where the cart was placed and that this adventure was being run into the ground. They didn't know what they were doing but wanted to convey that they did. Gratefully, people believed in me.

We developed a Board of Directors. Sister St. Patrick was on the board and a few other people joined on. We held a meeting about the truthful mess we were in and the reality of the bottom of the hole we currently sat in. Art who was the Executive Director, was fired. Sister St. Patrick suggested I fill the empty shoes. The Board of

Directors hired me to the be the new Executive Director of a treatment centre that was not yet.

I had a faith in Sister St. Patrick more than I did in myself, I think. I didn't really know what I was doing either, but I was always willing to learn. I agreed to this new role and said I would try. I trusted the people and specialists that advised us, like Sister St. Patrick that ran a detox centre, Dr. Dianne Hobbs, Dr. Joan Marshman and Dr. Brian Rush. I was aware of all of what I didn't know and rather than running around thinking I did and making misguided decisions, I would go to them... them that knew. I would always ask them for guidance. I had no idea what the full job description was of my new role but I was willing to do it and knew I had the strength and willingness to do so. Some people have a problem saying I don't know but I didn't. I simply leaned on my trusted resources.

Sister St. Patrick had a friend, Sister Mary Sharon in the community, who's brother was the executive assistant to the President at the Canadian Auto Workers Union (CAW). They had developed a program in their union for workers that suffered from chemical dependency and substance abuse and needed a place to refer their union members to. They were a powerful union and they put pressure the government for funding, along with pressure from Sister St. Patrick's friends at the Detox Centre. But the funding approval was stagnant.

By fall of 1985, we had put much effort in so many directions, but without the money, we would not actualize this dream. Defeated, I reached out to my friend Sister St. Patrick. I felt like I couldn't do anything further and all efforts were exhausted. We have done all that we could do. The work is all done. There is no more to put in motion. We have exhausted all of our resources.

I was ready to throw in the towel.

There was a retreat centre that the Catholic Church owned, and Sister told me to go there. She wanted me to go there or really anywhere, so that I wouldn't quit and would keep my faith in a divinely inspired initiative. She had a way of knowing what to do. I needed to stop obsessing about the funding. We had worked endlessly and tirelessly and while there was some encouragement and drips of dollars here and there, there were no decisions finalized. I am not good at just sitting around and waiting, so at her suggestion, I went for a week.

    I surrendered.

    It was me, a nun, a priest and a giant manor on the lake front of Lake Erie, in Port Burwell. I slowed down. I prayed. I meditated and my focus shifted. I liked it here. At the end of the week, I felt settled. An acceptance had washed over me replacing my frustrations. I now had the patience required to wait for the penny to drop, so to speak.

    Much to my chagrin, the government and funding was not happening at the pace of action I thought it should. Still, with nothing to do but wait, a few months later, my husband and I took a trip to Barbados. It was December of 1985. The weather was hot. A black-skinned Santa Claus was present for the holiday hype and it was paradise. I was out in the water, bobbing around in a raft when I got waved in to come to shore. I had received a phone call.

Sister St. Patrick had called and wanted me to return the phone call. With this vague message only, I looked at Dave and said "we got the funding!". He said "what do you mean you got the funding?" I told him I knew Sister St. Patrick would not be calling me in Barbados unless she had something important to say.

I was right. We got the funding. I called back Sister St. Patrick and she enthusiastically said "we are all set to go!" We had asked for money to open and run the treatment centre and we got it *and more.* The funding covered our operational costs. We received more than we even asked for. It was powerfully exciting.

I was feeling very divinely guided. I felt a trust in the guidance from Sister St. Patrick and I knew all would be okay.

I went back to bobbing around in the waters of Barbados, blissfully and gratefully.

After arriving back home, I learned quickly that if you are working for or with the government there is lots of paper pushing. Paper work on paper work, there was never a thing I would do without documentation. They knew little about our treatment centre, but had lots of paperwork on us.

I mean, if you went to the bathroom, you had it documented on paper. Nancy, who was Brian's wife had worked in a lawyer's office. She was the perfect Executive Assistant and she knew how to get it done.

We had a program developer from the government, come down to see what we were doing. She was no more interested in what we were doing in our program than flying to the moon, nor did she have any idea what we were talking about. But boy, she had it all written down on paper.

I began to submerge myself in education: addiction courses at the University, management courses and computer courses. My distaste for these stupid computer courses was on the same feeling level as cleaning my house. I didn't want computers in the centre, complaining that we didn't need them as we were people orientated. But they were all the rage and we got some. I never got one in my office but those working there did.

Once the funding came through, we fine tuned and further developed the programs. Latin Quarters was closing, so we bought all the pots and pans and dishes from my old boss. They were good and heavy and would last forever.

We were able to get good deals on some bedding from Canadian Linen and some paint and wallpaper from Color your World. We worked ten to twelve hours a day, seven days a week. I was at the Simpson Store shopping for the treatment centre, when I saw on a TV in the store, the Space Shuttle Challenger burst into flames and hurled towards the ground, 73 seconds after launch. Despite being so consumed with what we were doing, I have never forgot the end of that launch and its connection to birthing of the treatment centre.

Friends and volunteers came from all over, to paint, to put up wallpaper, to help clean windows and set up. It truly was a community collaboration to make it happen.

I was always on my knees praying for anything and everything. Mostly willingness, courage, faith and trust.

It is March of 1986; it is my fifteen years of living a spiritual life and in recovery from alcoholism. Dave and I recently moved to Chatham to be closer to the centre. Sister St. Patrick was staying with us and she and I were doing some recovery work, doing a personal inventory as I do every anniversary of my recovery. After dinner, I said to her "I've been thinking lately and I think my childhood had a bigger impact on me than I have realized." Sister St. Patrick never would tell anyone what she thought they should do. She preferred they figure it out themselves. Sister turned to me and said, "I have been waiting 15 years for you to figure this out. I wondered how long it would take?' She knew if people were working a spiritual program, they would find their way, when they were ready.

I continued to think about it a lot as time went on. I had no judgment but had a fuller awareness that I can't remember any warmth and affection as a child from my mother. She was good and did good things but her lack of emotion and tenderness, along with the fact that my loving father was away at war for 5 years, was on my mind. I started to see the past and its effects on me and my life and my spiritual dis-ease earlier before my recovery, in a broader light.

More so than ever, is also my understanding that there are two ways of living: a material life or a spiritual life.

A material life is an external focus. It is a concentration, on that which is outside of ourselves. It is placing the importance of our attention on how things appear, what we have in terms of belongings and on other materialistic possessions. An external way of living focuses on just that, external objects, people and situations. We may get caught up in what others think, say and ways they act. We spend time thinking or even obsessing, on how we believe they should be living their lives or how we think we might need to be "keeping up with the Jones".

On the contrary, a spiritual life is an internal focus. How we think, how we feel, and how we are behaving, which is independent from what others might be thinking, feeling and behaving.

I am learning that it doesn't mean that if you are more external focusing that you are in any way a bad person or that you aren't doing good things. You could be an amazing person doing brilliant things such as a scientist. You could be a kind and giving person but perhaps the spiritual goopity-goop doesn't connect with you, in this moment. But if you don't have something to free your spirit then there is less contentment and ease and more dis-ease. Externally focused living can leave people mentally treading water, kicking their feet and paddling in the waters of life vigorously or whatever the hell they have got to do, just to keep their heads above water.

Externally focused-living is more out of control. There are simply so many variables that are always changing. If our ease and peace depend on how the external world is responding or more so how we are responding to the external world, then we will flail through our days on a roller coaster of variability.

However, when we internally focus, that isn't to say we don't work with the external. We still have to take care of jobs and our homes. There is nothing wrong with wanting nice clothes or a spiffy car or to have the people in our lives feel happy or think like us, but if that is the focus of our happiness, again, we may feel fickle and our ease and peace fluctuating with the variables of our attention in that moment. I have learned if you are not practicing a spiritual way of living (reading inspiration, meditation, yoga, nature, praying, engaging with others spiritually, whatever!), your feet might land on the ground, but you will not feel the inner peace, that is attainable to you.

Nothing, I mean absolutely nothing, could convince me otherwise. When I was drinking and behaving, the way I was, before recovery, do you think I did that because I wanted to? I couldn't do anything with the mental obsessions, no matter how much I knew it would end up as a disaster, I still did it! I did not have the power or the tools to change. I had often obsessed about my failed marriage, the children I had left behind, the children I had not been there for, the enslaving thoughts and to drown my pain in alcohol. Before recovery, instead of turning it over to a higher power and connecting to spiritual health and a spiritual practice and a spiritual way of living, I was on a merry-go-round of pain, with no idea how to get off.

From that first day, 15 years ago now, that I went to my first recovery meeting and turned my life over to God and engaged fully into a spiritual practice, I never had the obsession to drink again. I fully emersed myself and after each interaction with this new way of living, I couldn't wait to get more, to read more, to meditate more, to surround myself in this spiritually recovery program.

It felt good to me, I yearned for it. I felt more ease, more connection, the love or whatever it was. It was nothing to do with whether I was a good person or not. It was everything to do with me living a spiritual life which was independent of any religious affiliation. You may have heard the saying, "Religion is for people who are afraid of Hell. Spirituality is for people who have already been there."

Many have had terrible experiences and difficult religious history within their families. This is very different. In the right company, I will joke about religion with friends, saying I am grateful to be protestant as my catholic friends feel guilty about everything in their "god-fearing" experiences. Joking aside, I felt glad to have gone to a united church. We may have drunk fake grape-juice wine but we weren't saddled down with guilt and all the rest of it, like many I knew.

There are others that don't believe in any religion or are even atheist. Which is fine, believe what you want to believe. A spiritual life is just believing in a power that is greater than yourself. Believe in spiritual fellowship, in the power of nature, something.

We are all given the will in our lives, to do what we will. If we live more internally, we won't get so darn caught up in the external world. When the satisfaction of our instincts for sex, security and society become the sole objects of lives, then pride steps in to justify our excesses. When we even simply look at the seven deadly sins of envy, gluttony, greed, anger, pride, sloth or lust, we can see the external focus. However, pride heads the procession, leads to self-justification and is spurred by unconscious or conscious fears. This is the basic breeder of most human difficulties and one of the main blocks to healing and progress. When we are fault-finding in others, we must turn our focus on healing ourselves by going within. Otherwise, the external focus of fault-finding of others and situations, will surely keep us stuck. It all comes down to self-examination, self-inquiry and self-regulation.

Fear, is at the base of almost all, for all human beings. When we have faith, we begin to replace the fear and then faith will take up more space. When I feel more fear, or more focus on the external, I know that I am lacking my attention in my own life and spiritual practice of going inward. When I go inward, with prayer, meditation, journalling or whatever, with that focus of how I am thinking, feeling and acting, then I nurture my feelings of more faith and simply, I feel more ease.

Those with fear of lack of money or with a focus on the material world, rob themselves of enjoying the material things that they already have. I often will inquire within when I am feeling outwardly focused and ask myself what is the worst-case scenario here? With my faith, I always had a knowing that I would be okay, no matter what the answer was to my query. Sometimes when I am afraid for something, I just pray and that feels better than just feeling afraid.

Faith gives me the power to know that through change or challenge, even when I am off the rails, I will be okay. It doesn't mean that I don't like my nice clothes or an aesthetic home, I just don't attach my well-being to them. With my spiritual practice, I can be at peace and have faith. This doesn't mean I like everything that is externally surrounding me, but I have no control or demand over how other people think or the attitudes that they may have. What I do have a lot of control over, is if I am listening to it or engaging in it.

No doubt about it, the disconnect in our world is from spiritual discord or absence of spiritual awareness within out selves and our own health.

It has been fifteen years since I started this journey and I know the foundation of my recover is a life of spirituality, of cleaning up the wreckage of my past and being on a spiritual journey. Many have not submerged themselves in it, like I have. I recall saying to Geri years ago, in regards to people that didn't submerge as deeply into as I did, "look what they are missing!" and she would calmly reply, they don't' know what they are missing, they've never had it.

It will sound odd, but not everyone is as lucky as I am: to have hit such a bottom as I did and therefore consequently had the recovery that I have had so far for the last decade and a half of my life.

Some can quit drinking or whatever external fixation that has consumed them and not live a spiritual life. From my experience, they do not have the level of peace comparatively. My friend used to say 5% to 10% get what they could have, some study a lot and are glowing, others not as much and they make some changes. One person is not a better person than the next. We all do it differently and other people can not be our focus. Our focus must be ourselves, our lives, our spirituality, whatever that means to us each, as individuals.

What I knew for sure is I was grateful. I love working with others and it certainly brings me joy. The more we work with others, when we are in service, the more satisfaction we derive. There is just no two ways about it, service is a part of recovery. Recovery, unity and service were part and parcel of success in my recovery and my life. There are no quick fixes or short cuts. It wasn't just about me quitting drinking, it was healing the soul. A great percentage of my well-being is to be in service. I am an extrovert and loved being with people and this made a distinct advantage for me.

People had made time for me when my trainwreck-self first landed at the station, and I sure as hell better make time for others and give back what I can. Whether it was getting the coffee made at a meeting or making sandwiches or simply greeting the newcomers with their trembling souls, to let them know they are welcome and they are loved and that I desire to help them as they need help...that is being in service.

Why is it important to be in service? When we have a spiritual awakening, it is important to try and carry it to others. Being active and committed to being there for those that need it. Being of service helps relieve the core problem of selfishness and self-centredness.

I had the ability to connect with people, not all, but most. Some for whatever reason, some were intimidated by me. I never understood it.

I recall one gal who I later became friendly with telling me this. This gal was in detox at the time and by her own words looking like the "wrath of God". She told me after she got sober, I had gone to the detox all dressed up, wearing a camel hair coat, leather boats and gloves, bouncing around, smiling and sharing about the recovery program that saved my life and all she thought was "who the hell does she think she is?" The ones that feel worse about themselves seem to feel more jealousy and intimidation.

My friend, Angus pulled me aside years ago when he saw this. I had been very involved, enjoying recovery and he said its wonderful all the things I was doing, but that I needed to understand that because I was so active and did as much as I do, there are going to be people that criticize me. He said, "but also know that if you don't do all you do, you will also be criticized."

In my earlier years, this would bother me. This would disturb me and I would wonder why people would criticize or be intimidated or jealous when I was doing this and that and trying to do all I can. Now, I understand that is their stuff and where they are at. I stopped being surprised or hurt to that extent years ago. I needed to keep being me.

Today, I stay focused, work my program, feel good about my thoughts and actions and live by my principles.

In April of 1986, Westover Treatment Centre officially opened its doors. We received funding from the Ministry of Health and Long-Term Care to open a residential alcohol treatment centre in Thamesville, Ontario. Myself, Brian Gallagher, Nancy Gallagher, Jovit Mendonca, and dedicated volunteers worked hard to establish this centre. We received funding for a 14-bed recovery centre. We hired a total of 12 staff members.

The Grand Opening event was spectacular. The Minister of Health was there and I had gotten to know her quite well along this journey and she was a lovely woman. There were many liberal government officials that had assisted us to open and the all the CAW union officials were in attendance too.

It was very exciting and this was a very big deal, to me, to have all involved as well as residences of our program, attend.

In 1987, I went and gave my hard-luck story to my buddy Dr. Brian Rush of the Addiction Recovery Foundation (ARF). He wrote proposals for funding and was considered a god as far as the Ministry of Health was concerned. We needed more beds to help more people so I asked him see if he could assist to get eight more beds for us. He replied he could make the figures and proposals do anything I wanted and he would make it happen.

He did it. Westover Treatment Centre received funding for 8 more beds for a total of 22 beds and we increased our staff to 28 team members.

It was wild and wonderful to be in the position I was. Not just the job I now held but my position as a human being in society. I am reminded of the promises that were made to me when I first got sober.

More experienced folks, would tell me years ago if I was painstaking about my development, I would be amazed before I was half way through. They would say I would know a new freedom and a new happiness and that I will not regret the past nor wish to shut the door on it. From time to time, I was still challenged by this. I did regret the pain I caused my children, particularly my daughter. She suffered as a result of the decisions I felt I had to make. I allowed their father to not follow the legal agreement. I let him do it. That is on me. I felt, and

I still do feel that the turmoil and chaos it would have caused to fight, would be worse for them.

I know drinking myself to death was not the solution to these regrets. I was grateful to be healing my soul sickness. "The eyes are the windows to the soul", they would often say. It made more sense now why years ago, when I looked in the mirror with despair that my eyes were dead, mere blank holes in my head. I am now so grateful that I understand that the drinking was a sheer symptom of a disease that created unconscious, deep depths of remorse. I can't go back and fix the past, but I am certainly doing everything I can, to be present now. The "old-timers" as we call them, promised that I will comprehend, the word serenity and I will know peace. I know this now.

We live in a quick fix society. Buy now, pay later. This includes our contentment. I continued, despite having a role of Executive Director of a treatment centre to work hard to learn, internalize and change my character defects. Growth would always be a part of this spiritual living scenario. I had to do the work still. My gift was a knowing to have the willingness to do it. If nothing changes, then nothing changes.

I had a gift by the grace of God, to understand the teaching from the mind. I did a psychological exam once, and got 94% percentile, on it with a summation that I should have been a psychologist. Sister St. Patrick would say, it was because I was willing to listen. I was thinking of going to university to become a psychologist but Sister would also tell me that I will waste years studying and not know much more than I do now, when I could be working and helping people instead. That made sense to me, so I let that thought go.

When I came into the new life, there were few women. Now there are hundreds of women with varied stories. Never mind how far down the scale we have travelled. I was sucking on a cheap bottle of wine in the market bathrooms, others drank in a more sophisticated and more socially accepted way. Some are low-bottom alcoholics not managing life and others were a high-bottom, still working, still socially decent attending high society events, while others yet were having seizures and delirium tremors or living on the streets. In my years of misery, powerless over the alcohol, the shame, remorse and fear, I was living in total contradiction to anything I would have thought I would stoop to, all the time, attempting to convince everyone I know I was okay. I had a disease that told me I do not have a disease! I need to remember this always, as many of us start feeling good with no more fear or guilt and then we cease the ongoing work required in our lives for a life that is fully and more peaceful.

Spiritual dis-ease was not selective to socio-economical status, education or good versus bad people. This is why I have respect, kindness and compassion for anyone that comes across my path or that steps foot in the treatment centre. When we take away all the labels, we are all just humans trying to get by.

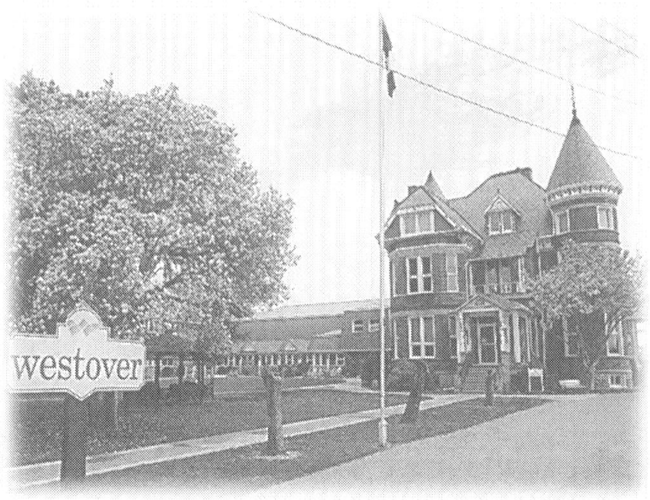
westover

Chapter 8

The 1990s

Nancy Gallaher had become a great friend. She was not alcoholic but she did have a spiritual dis-ease in her past from being a member in a household where there was alcoholism. She had an understanding of codependency, that I did not. I do not have a codependent personality but I understood that this dis-ease was a family dis-ease.

We presented a plan to the Ministry of Health for the Co-dependent or Family program at Westover. A program that is designed to help friends and family members recover from the harmful effects of living in a substance dependent environment. A program that would address the personality of a co-dependent individual, a 6-day resident stay to offer skills training on assertiveness, communication, defence mechanisms, and anger management, along with providing spiritual recovery. This was much different from the 21-day residential stay for the addiction programs.

In 1990, we established our Co-Dependence program. It was one of only two such programs available in Ontario. This was exciting groundbreaking healing for the physical, mental and spiritual health, of all involved.

My son David, has moved to British Columbia. Now in his mid-twenties he was seemingly enjoying life in the Rocky Mountains, working part-time at Earls restaurant as a waiter, and taking University courses.

It was March of 1992. Dave and I went to Florida for vacation. When we returned home from out flight and our drive from Detroit, we collected the mail. We were living in the country and had a mail delivery put on hold until the date of our return. When we retrieved the mail, it was thick and bundled up in elastics. As I sifted through the mail, organizing in junk, marketing, bills and so on, I was pleasantly surprised to receive a colorful envelop with a return address from British Columbia. It was from David. My birthday was soon. On the back of the envelope, he had written "this will be possibly the best birthday card you get this year." When I opened it up, a lovely birthday card but also a medallion in it that said "one month".

While I certainly knew that he drank a lot, so did a lot of folks in their twenties and in university for that matter. I could also recognize that he certainly had the symptoms of this disease. I didn't drone on or make too much noise about it. I had enough of a spiritual practice to know better than to focus on someone else and what I thought was right or wrong, even when it was my own son. I had said what I had to say in the past, and that was the end of it.

Despite all this, I did not know the extent of it. However, fortunately, David did.

A month prior to receiving this envelope, my youngest boy acknowledged his drinking was problematic and identified himself as an alcoholic. He had been sober for one month at this point, and sent me a medallion, scotch taped to my birthday card, with writing below it, "this one is for you mom."

He wrote me a lovely note stating that my love and influence was a guiding force to him and that the things I had said to him, or done for him and the people surrounding me and therefore him, had been an influential persuasion.

David shared that he had called around in Vancouver for a recovery program such as mine, and started to attend on a Tuesday, just as I had. Jokingly stating that "Tuesdays are the day people go to recovery programs".

I had been to Vancouver to visit him the year before. While there I had been to a recovery meeting during my time. I really enjoyed the people there. It was very much reminiscent of the one I had gone to when I first started going twenty-one years ago (and still to this day attend).

He ended up attending, the very same group.

In February of 1992, his father and I flew out to B.C., to help him celebrate the 1-year anniversary of his new lease on life. I am so grateful for my higher power, for spiritual recovery and life, for me and my baby boy.

The years pass in a blur, with long days and much effort at the centre and in recovery programs.

I loved it all. Dave was very active with volunteer work with the centre too. My kids and grandkids were doing well. The centre was a respite for the weary, providing healing options, should they embrace them.

My work and the work of others got the attention of the addiction world. The Addiction Research and the Thames Valley Addiction centre gave us many awards and recognition for the work we had achieved. The field of addiction usually does not receive much attention, but we got many folks paying attention. For this, I was very grateful.

I was first introduced to the Alcohol and Drug Recovery Association of Ontario in the beginning stages of Westover. The association was a non-profit organization and a hub of connection for the addiction industry. It was a big association which included all the treatment centres and recovery homes in the province. Over the years, I have been very active with this group, as the E.D. of Westover.

Recently, I was nominated and voted in as President of this old boy's club. Ironically, I had three influential women in my life that assisted this to happen. St. Patrick, Libby Murray (who was on the Board of St. Leonard's half-way house) and Dianne from the Addiction Research Foundation. I often felt to be riding off the coat tails of somebody that that supported me.

In 1996, the London YWCA awarded me with, the Woman of Distinction Award in Health and Technology. Astonishingly, Dr. Lauren McCurdy, who was instrumental in bringing the Ontario Breast Screening Program to London and was the first Regional Radiology Coordinator and a specialist in mammography, also won this award. More ironically and synchronistic to me, is that she was one the university students that rented a room from Dave and I, many moons before.

Crazy to me, was that I didn't know a thing about technology. Never had a computer in my office once. As far as I was concerned, I felt to me this is what I was suppose to be doing. I had surrender to something greater than me and it was divinely placed on my path. My higher power, the God of my understanding, put me in this moment and had a plan for me.

My friend Maude, would say "well much has been given Bevy, so much is expected." I knew whatever gifts I had, my higher power felt I could do, without being an egotistical maniac, what I have done. As long as I give the credit back to my higher power, I am okay. I didn't need to work on it and I never felt worthy of any of it.

I have been sobered for 25 years now. In my older age of this life, while I continue to attempt to live a spiritual life to the best of my ability, I have become increasingly aware that the more spiritual I become, the less I really know about it all. I mean I feel good. But while I continue to help and be of service to others (in which I believe I do a good job at), I was not spending as much time on myself and my own inventory as much as I probably should have been. Don't get me wrong, what I was doing was good and helpful for others, but I also need to remind myself to be mindful of my own character defects and my own life.

When I went within and when I allowed the quiet to fall over me, I dug deep into my inner being. I don't think I was conceited, but I was used to the positive interaction and acclaims that I received from my circles and from the new comers to the program, who thought that what I had to say, was gospel.

When you are told what a wonderful person, wonderful sponsor, wonderful program member, wonderful human being, wonderful this and that, you get used to it. You get used to hearing the praises and it can be easy to be remiss. The autopilot of positive gestures can overshadow the need to be truthful. Its important to do semi-annual or annual "house cleaning" of our lives.

This year, like every anniversary and now, after a quarter of a century, I do my inventory and I review my place in the seven sins. My lists have changed, evolved, expanded and minimized from the pages and page I once wrote. I don't judge, criticize or gossip, at least not out loud. I continue to work with my internal thoughts as I understand that gossip is a two-way street. I understand that small talk and judgment of others creates spiritual snobbery. So, I continue to attempt to practice mindfulness of thoughts. I have come to have a solid awareness that everyone has lived varied situations and has equally contrasting recovery experiences. It isn't good or bad, but just different. Each of us in different stages on this ride. I am reminded, again and again, to continue to worry more about what's going on between my ears and connection to my higher power and less about what others are doing, while continuing to serve in any way I can.

My brother Donnie, only in his early fifties has been struggling with his health. His ability to function has suffered for quite awhile. It was more of the same he had experienced most of his life: more back surgeries, more discomfort, more misuse and dependency of pain medication in attempt to control his physical distress and the cycle continued, as it has for many years. His dwarfism made any sort of back surgery management difficult for even the best doctors and the remedy and relief was minimal.

It was Thanksgiving weekend, and my brother was given a leave pass to attend my sisters home for the celebrations. He had to give himself intermittent catheterization as one of his new complications was inability to empty his bladder. Dave and I packed up all the necessary supplies that University Hospital provided and headed on our way to Tillsonburg. Donnie started to look more unwell throughout the visit. My niece Kelly was a nurse and had to assist him with his catheter and noted he was in rough shape. She assisted him to the bedroom to lay down. His color started to turn a bit grey and she said we should take him to the local hospital.

Jim, my brother-in-law who worked at the hospital called and told them we were coming. Dave was not a reckless driver by any means but knew he needed to get our dear Donnie to medical attention as soon as possible. The drive was pure agony for my poor brother. He was in much pain and overall seemed quite unwell.

He was taken to the ICU almost immediately after emergency room triage. While they were looking after him, I was talking to him. Nurses and doctors were scrambling around him and hooking him up to this tube and that hose. There was an urgency in the air.

That was the last time I talked to my brother.

He was in a coma from then on. An ambulance took him from Tillsonburg back to University Hospital the following morning. The medical team had put him in an induced coma, as his lung function was failing and his oxygen saturation levels were quite poor. We received the call that he had "coded" meaning his heart was trying to stop or did stop. They resuscitated him but he required life support to keep him alive.

Anne and I discussed with the doctors and agreed to a DNR or "Do not resuscitate" order.

Within the next few days, it didn't matter how much oxygen they gave him, his small lungs were not functioning as they should and his toes and fingers started to turn gangrenous black. The family, including his 7-year-old son would take turns at his bedside waiting and talking to him, despite his incapacity to reply.

It was Halloween 1996. Two weeks have passed and the reality needed to be accepted. He was only alive because of a machine breathing for him and even that was not very effective. Dave and I were one of the last to visit that night. I told my sleeping brother, its okay. Its okay to let go of a life time of struggle, its okay to let go of the pain and that I knew he was dying and if he is ready, its okay to go. I kissed his forehead and told him that I loved him dearly and Dave and headed home to Chatham.

As we arrived home and walked in the door, the phone was ringing. Seems it was the first time in his life my brother paid much attention to what I had to say, as he had let go. We put our coats back on and immediately headed back on the one-hour drive to University Hospital in London. We met Anne, Jim and Kelly there.

If I am to be honest, there was a sense of not only acceptance that my brother was gone, but of relief. He had suffered and been sick for so long, it was a blessing. I didn't want him just to stay "machine-alive" despite dying. He wasn't living, he was dying and dying itself, from my perspective is a whole lot better that staying on and suffering. I have a complete acceptance of what is, as it is.

I felt relief and I thanked God that he longer had to go on like that any longer and that his suffering was over.

By the late nineties, I was starting to think about retirement.

The Board wanted me to stay on but I was running low on enthusiasm and motivation and my ambition for new ideas for Westover were dwindling. I believe, people can stay too long. With a job like this, at a place like this, I think you need to have a leader that is enthusiastic and inspiring, for continued improvements and evolution.

We had just been accredited and recognized, as the best community-based treatment centre in the province of Ontario.

I thought *this,* is a good place to end off.

I am 65 years old now and resigned from my position of Executive Director at Westover Treatment Centre. I had been involved a lot with a volunteer association in Chatham, so the Board asked me look after the volunteers and public relations department. I thought this would be something I was capable of and enjoyed, so I agreed.

My role with this beloved treatment centre had gone full circle. I had accepted the new position, which was my original old job, upon coming aboard this adventure, back in 1984.

Frank, the new Executive Director was very educated and extremely qualified. It was the first time, St. Patrick and Dave disagreed. One thought he would be good for the job with proper guidance, the other felt he simply did not have the emotional and mental fortitude, as I did, for the job.

Frank leaned on me plenty in his new role and as long as I was around, things seemed to go fairly well for him.

However, not all is well, in my inner circle.

My dear, Dave has been diagnosed with cancer and we are making plans to move back to London, closer to the doctors and hospital. At 68, I retired again, this time from my new (old) position at Westover, to move back home to London and take care of my husband.

Chapter 9

Sister St. Patrick

By the Grace of God, I met Sister St. Patrick in 1975. A mutual friend Maude, introduced us. Well at least officially, as I, like many in this recovery life, had heard of her before. Everyone talked of her and apparently folks were talking to her about me. When we finally met, we weren't as impressed with each other as everyone thought we should be. She was the silent force and I was the fire cracker running around. But without hesitation, I easily conclude she was divinely placed on my path of life.

I was only a few years sober when this strong woman entered my life. She was very involved with alcoholism and detoxification and recovery. She was a Registered Nurse and she furthered her education and became a psychiatric nurse, with a special interest in the field of addiction.

The founders of this spiritual program worked with a Sister St. Ignatia and this special nun cared for thousands of alcoholics for decades of her life. Sister Mary Ignatia who passed in 1966, was beloved by all who were associated with or helped by her. She was often referred to as the "Angel of Alcoholics."

Sister St. Patrick modelled her special kindness for the wounded souls.   She worked with Addiction Foundation and became an honorary member of the recovery program, despite not being an alcoholic herself.

Sister St. Stephens recognized her ability to offer deep compassion and she had an ability to get them to do what they needed to do. There were no detox centres yet and the hospital emergency rooms would be doing everything they could to discharge alcohol cases out, while simultaneously, Sister St. Patrick was sneaking into their rooms to assist in any way she could. As such, she would be transferred to the various hospitals in London, Sarnia, Chatham and area. She became known for effectively helping alcoholics.

Sister St. Patrick was encouraged and mentored by Sister St. Stephen, when they were both nursing sisters at St. Joseph's Hospital. During this time, Sister St. Patrick became acutely aware that chronic alcoholic men were not being adequately served within the hospital system and often fell between the existing services. Fact was, not many women were known with this soul disease.

She became involved in the Detoxification Centre located on William Street, downtown London, which was officially opened on September 10th, 1973. It was a department of St. Josephs Hospital and St. Patrick was to be the director. She furthered her studies of addiction at Rutgers, a leading institution for addiction science in the United States.

Soon, as other detox centres sprouted up in the province, they would send the new directors down to be trained by Sister St. Patrick.

Folks marvelled at her connection to people with this spiritual affliction and her ability to understand.

Many just didn't understand the disease, even professionals. I still recall one time when I working at the Latin Quarter, meeting a man in the office who was training to be a medical doctor. Somehow the conversation became the subject of alcoholics. This doctor-in-training said "drunks are a waste of time, let them die". To which I piped up and said "I am very glad you were not my doctor when I was I the hospital due to my alcoholic drinking." I guess I didn't look like a "drunk" to him and he was unaware there is not a stereotype but a cunning and baffling disease.

Many medical professionals and people felt this way about "drunks". Not Sister St. Patrick. She knew more than most.

One time, Dr. Wareing, who delivered David and was a professor at the University asked me to help with other women that were troubled. Fact is, many including medical professionals didn't have a clue.

For whatever reason, Sister St. Patrick *did* have a clue. She understood and knew how to assist and guide people into a spiritual recovery. There was a comprehension she held that it was not a case of people just drinking too much but she recognized there was something beyond this.

Although there was not a lot of women in the program, she didn't love working with women. She thought men were much easier to support. I actually agree with her. But she did like me. We got to know each other and we seemed to share an innate knowing of alcoholism as a spiritual disease.

When my sponsor Geri was ill, Sister St. Patrick went up to see her in the hospital. Geri said to Sister "you will take care of her, won't you?"

When Geri passed, Sister St. Patrick and I became closer and closer. She was running the detox. Initially only for men, soon there after opened for women too. She would send the women after discharge to my meeting group and said "find Bev", and they would.

We became good friends and even collaborative partners. She trusted me. She would meet with the big car unions, GM and Ford to speak of assistance for employees and substance abuse programs in their companies. She would often drag me along, as she thought I could offer a good perspective to speak.

She was an advisor for spiritual direction. I respected her knowledge and understanding enough that when she spoke, I listened. I think she liked that I wasn't all "gaga" for her. She was a human being. I deeply respected her and her work with the Addiction Research Foundation.

When I received adulation and praise, she kept me grounded. She stayed true to her promise to Geri and assisted me to stay emotionally rooted and entrenched. Geri knew that it was a job and that no one could lead and guide me in like Sister St. Patrick could.

Within days of the idea of Westover, she was involved. She guided me, encouraged me and sat on the Board of the Treatment Centre.

She left the detox centre when she was 65 years old in 1987. Following this inspiration of Sister St. Stephen's, St. Patrick ran the St. Stephen's House, a Long-Term Recovery Home for alcoholics and addicts in the London area, the only one of its kind and was fully funded by the Sisters of St. Joseph, after she approached them. Initially, there were two homes and a soup kitchen.

She had a passion for helping those suffering from addiction winning one award after another from the police and the addiction foundations and so on. Sister St. Patrick understood spiritual healing. Despite being a nun, she knew the church won't keep people sober and clean but that they needed to develop a spiritual foundation and required healing of life. She'd say "They'd kick me out at the Mount" for talking this way.

She was tough, defiant and rebellious. You know the sweet little whispering nuns? She was not one of them.

Addicts and alcoholics would run circles around most nuns and the nuns would kill them with kindness. Not her.

Her Mother Superior would haul her in, for her defying ways. It didn't phase or bother her. She wasn't disrespectful, she just knew something different or perhaps more.

She had been a pro tennis player and was a larger athletic set woman. She loved sports and was highly competitive. One time, on the Westover fun ball team, she cut our good friend Marilyn, for "not being good enough". She hated to lose.

I would call her "Patty" in private, but in public it was Sister St. Patrick, to show the respect to her that she most definitely deserved. She was more attached to me that her *Sisters*. We had a special bond. She loved when I would go to church with her, "bouncing around, up and down" like Catholics do.

She was strong and tough and full of opinions and gave just the right amount of guidance to folks. But she was also smart enough with a knowing that folks needed to figure out somethings on their own, to conclude with their own personal insights. I still recall my 15th sobriety birthday and sharing with Patty that I thought I was having a revelation that my childhood had a greater impact on me that I was aware and her wondering how long it would take. She knew on some topics, that if people were working a spiritual program, they would find their way, when they were ready.

She occasionally indicated to me that she didn't think I understood or appreciated that I was very blessed and had been given the gift of God's presence in my life. I believe we all have a presence in our lives but apparently some of the Godly experiences I have encountered, are not common place.

Sister St. Patrick would say, "Did it ever occur to you that these are rare occurrences not everyone has?" I suppose I didn't. She would explain, as a Nun she doesn't and many in the church don't.

After 25 years of friendship, I could see she was getting older and weaker. I knew she was sick. You could tell. Soon, she was diagnosed with cancer. Despite, there was a faith, that things would be okay.

She asked me to come to St. Stephens home and assist her two to three days a week. I was still volunteering and doing the Public Relations and fundraising for Westover but this was manageable. Sister St. Patrick was concerned about the men's house. She wanted the new Executive Director of Westover to take over running it, but he had no interest in taking that on. There was worry that the St. Joseph's Sisters would shut it down.

In 2000, as Sister St. Patrick became more ill and unable to continue her ministry, Dave suggested "maybe Bev would run it." So, I assumed the role of manager of this men's recovery home and was out of retirement, working full-time, once again.

I was used to having all the players in the game. I had many working in different divisions at Westover. Now, a solo show and I had many doubts. I said to her, "I don't think I could do this like you." The low rock bottom alcoholics weren't scared of me. They were with her. She said, "The world doesn't need another Sister St. Patrick, it needs you. You go there and you do you. She gave me confidence. She didn't say things, to just say them. She truly believed in me.

I filled the position as a volunteer and I was glad to do it. I was not motivated by money. If I didn't like it, I thought I won't do it. Soon after, the Nun's wanted to give me a small amount, so I accepted that.

Sister St. Patrick's body became more taxed and tired. She was unwell or unconscious most of the time. She asked for me to do her Eulogy. I was honored.

Her passing was not tragic, but a blessing. She wanted to die and go to heaven.

The day of her funeral was a celebration of her life. I have never been one to write down my words when I speak but instead pray for guidance. The huge cathedral chapel at the Mount of St. Josephs was packed with Priests, Cardinals, Bishops and about 50 nuns and nurses, friends and many, many people that she had assisted in her life. I found it a bit amusing with this large hierarchy of Catholic officials, that perhaps one of them might be better qualified. It was a Catholic funeral and run accordingly, but the Eulogy was a Celebration of Life, my friend's life. There were many recovery people there. I made a joke that I wasn't used to speaking in this part of the church but rather used to being in the church basements for meetings. Those that knew what I was speaking of, chuckled.

Her commitment to the field of addiction was astounding and she was indeed celebrated. The sisters lined up as they took the casket outside. The pall bearers were men in recovery and my Dave. She always did like him.

The kind praise came from many in regards to my words about this woman. I could feel myself ponder, "How the hell did I get here?" I felt so fortunate and honored to be asked to offer her tribute. I would remind myself that I am on this path for a divine reason and when I was running the show myself, before recovery, my gifts were not so obvious. I thanked my Higher Power.

I know she was one of the people put in my life for a purpose. When I got credit for things I had done, I would remind myself that Sister St. Patrick, along with others, were on my path and put in my life to guide me and give me the confidence to do the things I needed to do. People, such as "Patty", opened the door for me, so I was able to do what I do.

The sisters needed to give up on supporting the house and were unable to do it anymore. Mostly due to the fact that there were no more sisters to run it, as the number of people becoming nuns were meager and scant. The St. Joseph's sisters gave the house and donated about twenty thousand dollars. The government wouldn't fund the recovery home which was fine really. St. Patrick would have wanted us to continue to have our own autonomy. The government knew little about addiction and a whole lot about paper work. Government involvement worked for Westover as we had a lot of staff to do bureaucratic paperwork and deskwork but this home had no staff but myself.

Officially, in 2004, St. Stephen's House of London was turned over to Turning Point Inc., for the sum of one dollar, with the provision that I continue in my role. Sister St. Patrick would be okay with this.

Higher Power doesn't come down and give us breakfast in bed, but I believe there is a powerful synchronicity and an alignment of people, places and things provided. I have often said that it takes an army and that there is a cast of a thousand.

Sister St. Patrick, without doubt, was one of the lead actors.

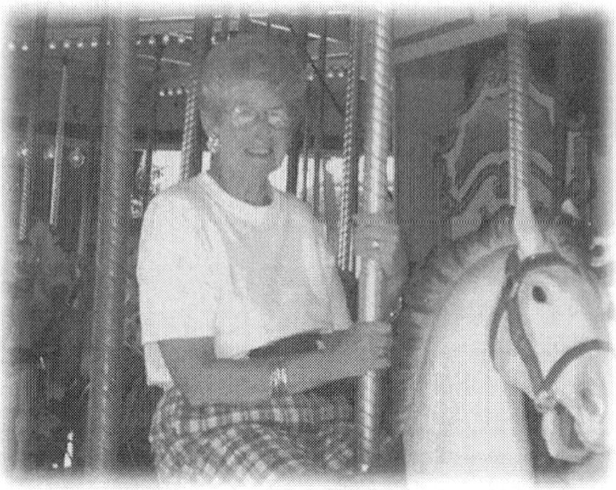

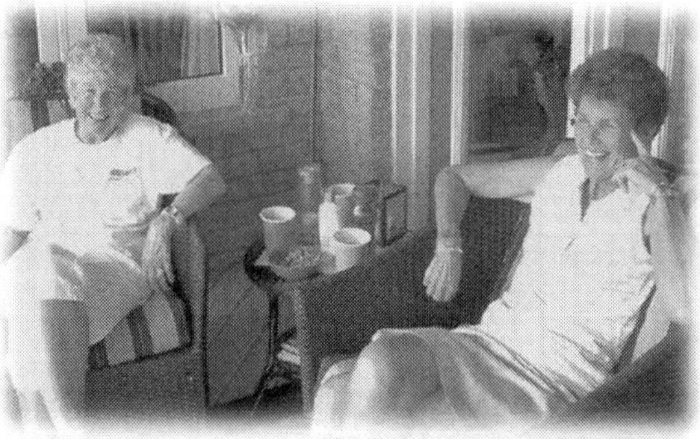

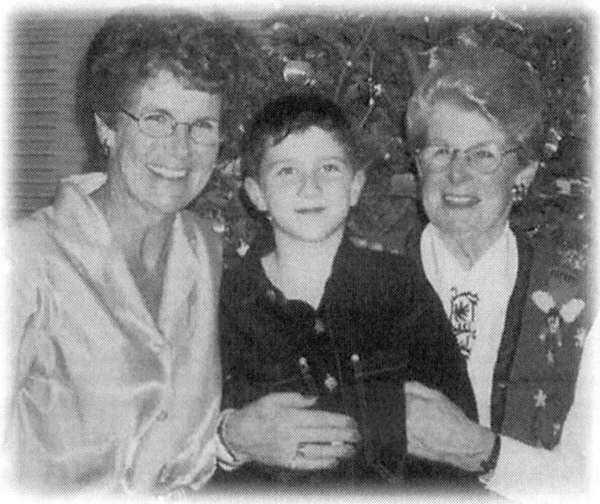

Chapter 10

The 2000s

Dave has been receiving his cancer treatments and doing well as can be expected. His recovery is good and the prognosis is hopeful

Relief.

However, Frank, the new Executive Director at Westover, is not managing well and the prognosis for his position is poor. My move away and my lack of support didn't fair well for him. He had become emotionally exhausted and unable to cope. Sadly, Frank began to be paranoid and dysfunctional. Recovery was what he needed and ultimately, he was let go from his position.

The Board asked me to come back for two to three weeks, while they sorted things out. The staff was absolutely spent from dealing with the situation. All of this, is a direct contrast of what is conducive for staff at a treatment centre. They needed to be centred and grounded themselves. The staff needed to be emotionally, physically, mentally and spiritually stable individually to be able to work with clients of addiction and their suffering souls.

So, I agreed.

My two-to-three-week stint to help out in the interim, driving back and forth from London to Thamesville, had me back as the Executive Director of Westover…again!

The Board of Directors continued to look for an E.D. but they were looking for someone like me. I say this, not in an egotistical way, but I was a package deal. Not only did I have the personality and the mind to do the job, with me, came Dave. My husband took charge of the alumni and maintenance and other volunteer programs that were crucial to Westover. There wasn't going to be another E.D. that could do that. We ultimately were a one of a kind, two for the price of one, special deal.

In reality, an Executive Director wasn't meant to do all that I and Dave did as a team. They had to revamp things. They needed to adjust their expectations.

They finally hired an ex-priest for the job. He had left the priesthood to marry. His name was

Willy. If I am to be honest, he never sat well with me, but I wasn't on the hiring committee. Many people in the community thought he was a good man and a good find.

Willy tried to run Westover like the Catholic Church and he damn near ran into the ground. In my opinion, to run Westover you need to have the identifying experiences. Meaning, Willy knew nothing about working with addictions and well, we alcoholics are a different breed. Part of running the treatment centre that is crucial, is having the alumni come in and volunteer, share and work with the residence. He turned them all off and in no time, no alumni were willing to volunteer at Westover any longer. He was an egotistical and arrogant man. They asked me to stay another month, to assist him with his transition into the position and show him the ropes.

The first Monday morning I drove down there to assist, I started working with him at 9am and by 10:30am he told me to go home. He pats me on the back and told me that he had it all covered. Can you imagine the arrogance of sending home one of the founders of the centre, that had retired and come back over and over and after less that two hours into orientation of your new job, thinking you knew more?

So, I went home and I *retired* for the third time from Westover, when I was 70 years old.

However, I still was managing St. Stephens Recovery Home for men, initially starting a few days per week, but now running the place 5 days a week. I certainly am missing my friend St. Patrick. There is an appreciation that I have for her now. I mean I always appreciated her but there is a deeper recognition and gratitude for her and simply how richly blessed I was to have her in my life. She cared profoundly for me, and I, for her.

This one fellow that would often end up at the detox on weekends would teasingly quip that his version of a "spiritual awakening" was him landing in the detox and on Monday morning Sister St. Patrick driving up to take him to St. Stephens. She certainly had a way.

When I am feeling challenged, I am reminded of Sister St. Patrick's confidence in me. "Just go and do you, it works!" she had said. If I didn't know anything, one thing I knew for sure was that she had never said anything that she didn't believe fully. She never said things to people, to just make them feel good. She spoke her truth with conviction. Her faith in me, and my ability to do this, boosted my faith in myself.

St. Stephens Rehabilitation home was immersed in a spiral healing and recovery program. The "rules" of home were changed through the years to make it more conducive for successful recovery. They had to go to detox. They had to find a sponsor and go to regular meetings of recovery. These men were given life-skills rehabilitation for two months with no work and then they could phase back into their workplace. Some needed extra time. We would work with the big companies and factories and their substance abuse team to assist these men to establish firm foundation in recovery and life skills. Some didn't know how to shop, clean and take general care of themselves.

They were required to participate in a spiritual recovery program and they were encouraged to stay out of the churches. St. Stephens was a place to have time to heal, shift and reconsider or learn life-skills. Not all need a home like this, but some do. Many, especially drug addicts, needed to root down, find foundation and learn how to live. Finding roots instead of aimlessly travelling through life with no direction. Many were good souls but were not feeding their souls. St. Stephens was a valuable piece of recover but it was no replacement for a spiritual program.

Sister St. Patrick often used to say to the men, "Stay out of the churches. The church didn't help you get sober in the first place and isn't going to get you sober. Maybe in time, it will help keep you sober, but for now you need a spiritual recovery program."   She told me once, that if the Superiors at the Monastery knew what the heck, she was telling these men they'd throw her out of the community. Imagine a nun, telling people to stay out of the church.

Times were changing and spiritually and church were not parallels and people were understanding this more. I made small changes, but generally ran the place just how St. Patrick had it running it, as it worked.

One of the greatest things taught to me, is to do for others, to be in service. Many of us, caught in a spiritual disease become so selfish and self-centred, we forget this. But giving to others and helping others is one of basis for living a spiritual life. I felt fortunate that I liked it. It was part of my nature.

I would often encourage the men to call someone and offer assistance in any way they can, to forget about themselves for fifteen minutes, to get out of their heads and stop thinking about themselves for a bit.

Doing kind little things, rather than bitching and complaining can be a very powerful tool to shift life experiences into a healing experience. When we get in that complaining mode whether it is about the awful things someone did to us ten years ago, or that someone left only a few drops in the bottom of the milk container, it is still complaining. Instead of grumbling about the few drops someone left in the bottom of the milk bag and bitching about the smallest injustice, just empty the milk bag, put into a new one and get on with life. There is no need to run around talking about what you have had to do. It's the small things as much as the big things. It's as simple as that.

Just like in any home, St. Steven's had to have order and direction. Sometimes, it was encouraging services and kindness to one and another. Other times, it was putting your foot down to explain what was acceptable or unacceptable, in regards to the paths of healing. We can't have people acting out all the time. Sometimes they needed attention, so I picked my battles. I had to be okay with making mistakes, teaching them that mistakes don't need to lead you into a tail spin. Foundation was necessary. St. Stephens home provided that.

Still active in the community as well, one woman I know who I had talked with was trying to get clean and sober again. She had a lot of past traumas from childhood and was now was the mother of four kids but unable to provide properly for them. She knows she should be taking care of her children but doesn't know how. Heck, she can't take care of herself as this disease has a tight grip on her. Children's Aid is involved now. A friend of mine in the program brought her to see me, again.

I told her straight forward that if she didn't start doing what she needed to do, to take care of herself and get herself straightened away, she won't need to worry about her children, because they're not going to be hers. Her eyes bugged out. I said to her "You have been to see me now three times, and I have listened to you talk about your father three times. I get it. I get what happened to you. But I don't want to hear one more word about your father. The jig is up. Time for you to take action. Forward, future action."

She left my place and went back to the women's home she was staying at. Apparently, she told the other women that they might want to think twice about going to see Bev. *"She is not as nice as everyone says she is."*

But if you don't know, you don't know. If your soul is sick, it won't get better if you don't start letting it heal. If you don't start doing something different than what you are doing, then nothing will change. We can get caught up in this, even lost.

When you stop doing the destructive things that are continuing to hurt you (and those around you), whether it's replaying memories, blaming external situations or blaming your past for your behaviors in the present, or drinking yourself to death – when you can address and stop doing the destructive things you are doing and heal it, you can laugh at yourself for doing them, and that's when you know there is healing of the soul.

My friend Butch, often jokes about this. He says that when he speaks, he shares how he had bought a brand-new Cadillac at 10am and by 6pm he had it wrapped around a pole and everyone laughs including him. Its not that it was funny when it happened but to be able to recognize the destructive behaviors and jokingly banter about it, now that we are "awakened", is spiritual awakening. It is soul healing.

I continue to share my experiences with others, so that they may be able to relate and identify. It assists others to see ways for problem resolutions and alternative options for a better life. Lead by example. We all need to relearn and release the dysfunctional processes we may be caught up in. We can get trapped in the pain or the replaying of stories. Sharing experiences allows others to stop and receive an option for change. Stopping the drinking, the drugs, the sex, the codependency, the whatever-addiction is only the first step to this process. The real work starts and continues after that, building or perhaps re-building the soul.

Clean house and take inventory of yourself. Honest, real inventory. Trust in something bigger than yourself. Have faith. Be of service to others by giving back. These are foundational tools. We can spend so much time blaming, criticizing and judging others, by continually focusing on the outward. The foundations of spirituality allow us to go within, to have the means to quiet ourselves and empower ourselves through the acknowledgement of what we can and can not control.

Does that mean we still don't have problems or get upset? Of course not, at least not for me. I still get challenged when things don't go the way I want. I still get annoyed with little things that I don't like. At times, I can still get into black and white thinking, my way or the highway. But it is less often, less in duration and I am much more self-aware. Continuing to counsel others to guide their spiritual program, I do so effectively as my emotions are not involved. I can detach in a healthy way to offer objective perspective. That's not always as easy when it is personal. I have better connection to my spirit, with more effective soul-searching techniques, giving me healthier solutions. That is growth. That is spiritual progress.

That is the power of spiritual healing and what differentiates it from religion. Spirituality is made for everyone, for every spirit. It doesn't matter what you believe in or don't believe in. It is a higher power of each individuals understanding.

Sister St. Patrick used to tell me that I don't need to be taking any courses, and just continue to share and sponsor. That is one piece of advice of hers, that I didn't listen to.

Anything or any course to do with addiction and my role in the addiction field, I took it. I took more damn courses, than Carters has pills. Courses on addiction management, rational self-counselling, life skill management, relapse prevention, and on and on and on. You name it, I took it. I'd go to them in Toronto, at Western University... wherever they had them. They cost a small fortunate. But I couldn't get enough of them.

Through this, I had become good friends with Dr. Martyn Judson. I had a lot of respect for him and he, to me. He was on the Board of Directors at Westover and was an expert in the field of addiction. Dr. Judson ran groups for professionals afflicted with alcoholism or addiction – groups for doctors and nurses, lawyers, teachers, business people etc. In lots of cases, professional people are snobs. They felt they were too good for a recovery program. But with Dr. Judson, they felt more dignified attending the classes and groups of the acclaimed and highly regarded doctor.   After a while, he would tell the professionals, that they should go down to the Tuesday recovery meeting and find Bev T., "she knows more about this than any of us". Many would.

I don't share this to be arrogant, I was just doing what I was suppose to be doing, with humility. I went to my Tuesday meetings weekly, greeted people at the door, shared my story, listened to others. These were the rules of recovery, taught to me.

Everyone liked Dr. Judson. He held more knowledge about addiction in his little finger, then anyone else had in their whole body but also possesses more humility than most. He is an addiction doctor that studied all over the world – Manchester, England, somewhere out on west coast, and Simon Fraser. He is assistant professor of Psychiatry and Family Medicine at the University of Western Ontario. As well, he continues to be the Medical Advisor to the Westover Treatment Centre and is certified in the Management of Drug Misuse by the Royal College of General Practitioners (UK) and the International Society of Addiction Medicine.

He has produced several television documentaries regarding the treatment of alcohol and drug addiction.

Dr. Judson is probably the best addiction doctor in the province and has done so humbly, modestly and unassumingly. I think that is why we get along so well; an eagerness to learn and a humble disposition.

Addiction Services of Thames Valley named me a "person of the year" at their annual meeting. They asked me to speak and then honored a group session room or something in the building, with my name attached to it. It felt a little dubious, as I was well known to be a good member in recovery with a spiritual program, which included abstinence. This place embraced harm reduction or controlled drinking, in which "problem drinkers" reduce their alcohol intake but don't necessarily embrace abstinence, which was a rare and controversial approach in my recovery world. Regardless, I was honored and am reminded to not judge or criticize what others are doing but mind my own business and to continue to live my way of spiritual recovery.

I enjoyed my role at St. Stephens and loved that my Dave was the home's maintenance man. I don't know a tap from a drill, and had no interest in learning about it. Dave knew a lot of folks and had a lot of connections in the home building and maintenance world, making contacts through the years, so he always knew who to call if we needed repairs, if he couldn't take care of himself.

We were independently run which meant we had no money and I spent a lot of my time fundraising and doing public relations, something I loved to do and was good at it. This brought me back full circle to my roots and original role twenty plus years ago at Westover.

Dave started an annual St. Stephens fundraiser golf tournament and I started an annual walk-a-thon. My friend John Webster knew many big pockets at many big companies in the city such as Don Ellis and the President at Labatt's, and he would often come through for us.

People would joke, "I don't know how come we gave all that money. Bev started talking to us and before we knew the cheque was signed." Despite being in our seventies, there was no desire to stop being at St. Stephens. I did what Sister St. Patrick told me to do and it worked. These men needed assistance to learn basic skills; to make a meal, to clean up dishes, to make a bed, and all the other basic responsibilities of a home. Most have never lived a normal way of life. I made sure they got to meetings, that they got a sponsor and learned about a spiritual life. I did counselling and sponsorship. Sponsorship meaning to hold space, to see them, to hear them, to be there for them and to really listen to them.

One thing I can declare, is that most folks say that I am a very good listener. Anybody can tell you what to do. Listening, however is an acquired, nurtured and celebrated skill.

Chapter 11

The 2010s

St. Steven's is running tickety-boo, as smooth as a recovery home can. My family, my children, my grandchildren are seemingly doing well. My Davey started to facilitate regular fundraiser Bingo nights and life is good.

I like working with these men and I continue to enjoy sponsoring many women. I will sponsor and assist almost anyone willing. When I say willing, I don't mean just because they have reached out to me but rather those that want help. I am not interested in spending time with those not willing to do the work.

I have devoted and immersed my time and life to recovery, in one way or another. Would I have done it that way again? Who knows, but this is the way it has unfolded. Not all want to do what I have done. That is okay. It's not like I thought "all I want to do in my life is look after people and pass on what I learned". The spiritual recovery program's purpose is to assist the suffering soul to heal, prepare us to go out into the world and into society and serve a useful purpose.

My useful purpose just happened to be, to assist others with the soul-sickness of alcoholism.

I can remember being a year and a half sober, working down at the Latin Quarter and John (the owner) would delegate me to talk with staff that were sick. He would let me use his apartment to take them to meet with them. I simply had a way from a very early time in my recovery. It just seemed to be, the way my life unfolded. I had never thought or desired for it to take me where I am today. I simply put one foot, in front of the other. My higher power had a purpose for me.

I have never felt superior or that I was better than, as a result of all this attention. But I got it, none the less. If I let this kind of stuff go to my ego, I certainly wouldn't be able to have done what I have in my life. If I had, no one would be saying "go talk to Bev", they'd be saying "stay away from that ding bat!"

I contracted shingles. I went to my family doctor, who was a lovely woman, for examination. During the assessment, she found a lump on my breast.

Long story a-whole-lot-shorter, I had cancer.

I can't tell you why, but I didn't feel upset or concerned about it. I just wasn't. Dave and my family are much more troubled than I. I simply trusted my higher power and prayed for acceptance, had faith and prayed daily.

I was sent to an Oncologist and they took a biopsy. It was an aggressive type of breast cancer and they operated to remove the lump quite quickly. At my age, chemotherapy was deemed not suitable and recommended radiation as treatment following my surgery. All the cancer doctors and team at the Regional Cancer Clinic were amazed that I was always in good spirits and seemed healthy otherwise. I suppose not all respond the same way I do to a cancer diagnosis and treatment plan, as the medical team seemed impressed that the whole ordeal wasn't throwing me into a loop.

I believe myself to be honest, when I say I simply wasn't concerned about the treatments or the condition.

Dave drove me to my first few radiation appointments. I had zero side effects. I was never sick and I felt just fine. I thought this is ridiculous for Dave to be driving me to these appointments, he has better things to do than drive me around. Therefore, for the next several weeks I drove myself to clinic for radiation. I had healed easily from the surgery and the treatments didn't hurt me at all. I was told there could be common side effects such as fatigue, soreness, swelling and skin irritation. I had none.

After my treatments, I would drive over to work at St. Stephens. I went all day, every day. I don't mean to be glib, but I never felt sick, not from the cancer nor the treatments. Therefore, life carried on after my daily clinics for radiation.

The mind, body and spirit are so powerful and are always communicating. Perhaps my connection to my higher power and to my spirituality kept me feeling good, physically, emotionally and mentally. I truly don't know.

Health is health. It's not just your physical, it's not just your emotional or mental, it's not just your spiritual. It's a package deal, and health is health.

I don't think you can think your way out of serious illness but I think that the reason I fared so well and wasn't weakened, as many others receiving treatments and many at a younger age than I, was my strong spiritual practice and I am not afraid of dying.

The doctors and nurses would marvel at my good moods upon arrival for treatments and appointments. My doctor was amazed at my disposition and mindset saying it was a rarity. I trusted in God's plan for me.

I had been much sicker in my past and certainly if there was a time that I should have died, it was back in 1971 when was I was so sick and crazy and when my husband would have to pound on my body, as I was literally drowning from drinking so much and so fast. I have no groans or worry. I should or could have died all those years ago when I was drinking myself to death and wondering how much longer I was going to have to live this way. But I didn't and have lived an exceptional life.

Friends would comment they kept forgetting I had cancer as I didn't talk about it. I just never felt the need to. Now, I am mid-eighties and have been given a life of blessings. There was no need to fuss about this.

The surgery and treatments were successful. The doctor told me that with the type of cancer I had, it would return somewhere down the road but given that I am in my mid-eighties now, I will probably leave this world before it happens.

Then it was over. I was given the "all-clear", I hit the gong at the clinic, we all celebrated and that was the end of all the fuss.

I didn't give it any more thought.

A few years have passed, I am happy and well. My friend Alec C., who sat on the Board of Directors of St. Stephens was one of the most down to Earth people ever, despite coming from quite an affluent family. He was retired and looking for things to do, and did volunteer work. He and Bill S., who was an accountant and the Chair of the Board, got along well and worked nicely together. Alec, was up to no good.

One day, he handed me a big folder to let me know what he had been up to. It was a giant folder of me. He had been gathering and collecting information about my work as a volunteer director at St. Stephens over the last many years. There were newspaper clippings, award information and letters written from people that were influential people, such as Dr. Judson and so on. As I got a little into the folder, I was bored of reading this stuff about myself. Alec had put forth a nomination to the Governor General of Canada for an award for me.

I carried on a bit before going along with it all. I scolded him that I didn't need any award and I was doing all this for Sister St. Patrick and I enjoyed it and this wasn't necessary, blah, blah, blah. Then I didn't give it anymore attention.

Until that nomination, became an award.

I received a letter in the mail, dated September 28, 2017 and it was from the Governor General of Canada announcing my success of nomination and an invitation for a fully paid trip to Ottawa for me and my family, to receive the award.

So, with gratitude, Dave and two of my children Cathy and Rick and I got on a plane and went to Ottawa. My David would have been there but he had moved to the U.K.

They picked us up at the airport in a fancy car and took us to our hotel. I couldn't believe it. The Lord Elgin Hotel, located in downtown Ottawa, just a stone's throw away from the Rideau Canal was a luxury hotel built in 1941, but that wasn't the amazing part. I had been here before. In fact, when I was a young teen, my father's cousins took me there and it was the first time I had ever been in a hotel. It was fancy and had a pool indoors and all the amenities which was quite a site in the mid to late 1940s, especially for a gal from the little town of Iroquois.

What a lovely synchronistic event.

The fact is, it was Dave's research that got me sober, Geri's sponsorship that kept me in check, this spiritual recovery program that allowed me to maintain sobriety and Sister St. Patrick's guidance and faith in me that lead me to where I am.

I also had the "personality" for the job. Jovit, one of my Westover founding friends had told me years ago about the personalities of recovery.

He joked that the founders of the recovery program talked about the different personalities in recovery and those that would do well and help others, and if there were a picture beside the description it would be mine. I just had the constitution, by the grace of God to do what I do. It has nothing to do with me but the gifts I was given and only with the credit of my spiritual program. So, I wasn't as nearly impressed about the award, as the rest of them.

Although I did enjoy that we're attending Rideau Hall at 1 Sussex Drive, the official residence in Ottawa of both the Canadian monarch and their representative, the Governor General of Canada. Honored as I was, the one man that I really would have loved to have seen and met, was absent. But I guess Prime Minister Trudeau was too busy that day.

Kidding aside, I was glad to have my family there with me. Dave S. and Alec was able to sneak into the event and attend, as they had family that worked in the Governor's office. My husband and my children were there and that meant something.

There were several people there receiving various awards.

Kate Young, a member of parliament, representing London, Ontario, rose to her feet and said:

Mr. Speaker,

Today I rise to acknowledge Beverly Thomson, a London West resident and recipient of the Governor General's Sovereign Medal for Volunteers.

As an official Canadian Honour, the Medal for Volunteers recognizes the exceptional volunteer achievements of Canadians from across the country.

Beverly Thomson has spent many years helping those suffering from alcohol and drug addiction. She was a founding member of Westover Treatment Centre in Thamesville and volunteer Executive Director of St. Stephens, a recovery home for men in London.

After decades of devotion to get local and affordable treatment programs in place for people battling alcohol and drug dependency, Bev Thomson is still championing addiction awareness today.

Thank you, Beverly, for the lives that you have touched, and for all that you have done for

Southwestern Ontario. Your selflessness and dedication to service is truly an inspiration

Thank you, Mr. Speaker.

And that was that. I received the award, got some wonderful pictures with my proud family and had a luncheon at Rideau Hall.

I just turned 85 years old. Its now April of 2018, and the time is right. I had been waiting for my good friend Kevin to turn 65 years old and retire. He was perfect for the job. I felt healthy and bright but the time was right for me to retire from this gig. Kevin needed to be financially capable, with his pension in place to step in to this role. I knew he would be wonderful at the new Executive

Director of St. Steven's. Now, he is prepared to step up, as am I, to step down.

They had a big party for my retirement at St. George Church. The place was packed with familiar faces ranging from many family members to many, many people in recovery. There was good food, lots of reminiscing and memories shared and some very loving, thoughtful speeches.

They gifted us, Dave and I, as my husband was such a big part of St. Steven's as well, a River boat European Cruise.

What a gift!

A few months later, we flew to Amsterdam. My youngest and dear son David and his partner Clive joined us on the cruise, from Amsterdam to Frankfurter.

Other than poor Dave getting confused and lost at the airport, the whole trip was just the most wonderful time. I am feeling very fortunate and grateful for my friends and their gift, the trip itself, my family and my life.

I am officially-officially, for-real this time, retired. I will continue to go to meetings, talk and sponsor women wanting help and spend time with my family and friends. I have never done well with taking it easy, but I trust all will be well.

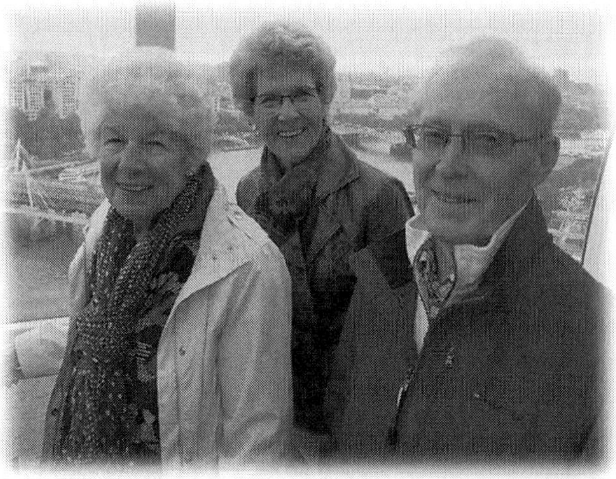

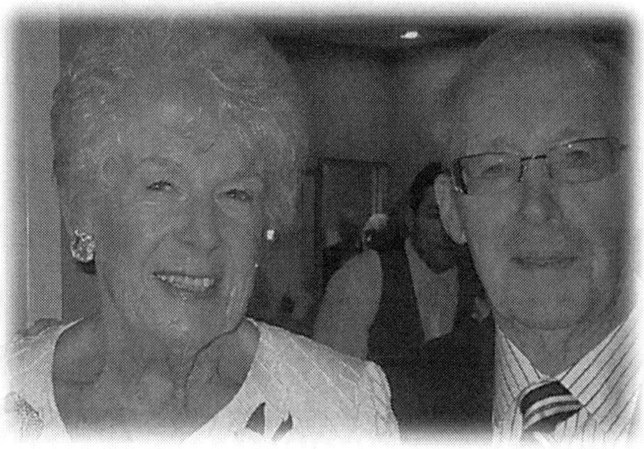

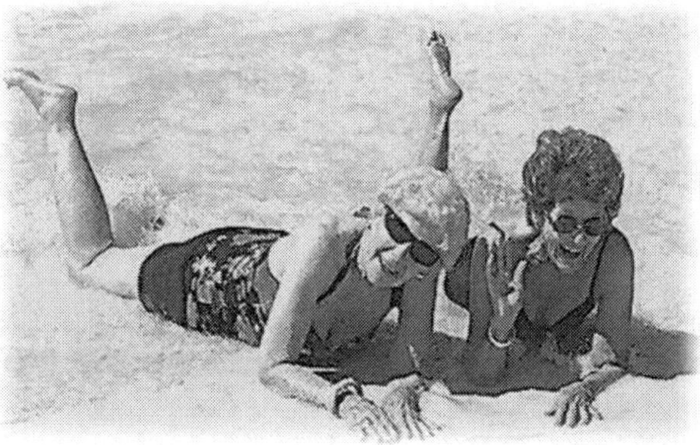

Chapter 12

The 2020s

I have not been truly a part of a global experience such as this, since the war. Here we are, being told to stay in our homes and away from others due to a worldwide, all-encompassing contagion. I don't have a problem following rules and I trust in the medical and science community, so I did what I what I was told to do.

Clive, David's long-time partner, is a scientist working with Oxford University in the U.K., on vaccine development for the coronavirus. When I hear the varied theories out there, I simply turn to him for truthful and factual advice.

Dave and I were accustomed to doing video-chats or *Zoom* or whatever the heck they are called, with David and Clive. We talked weekly and timed it accordingly with the time difference to Wales. As of late, I started talking more this with way with family and friends, since we can't be together.

I just finished a zoom meeting with my recovery fellowship. If you had asked me fifty years ago, that at the age of 87 years old, that I would be gathering with people virtually, I would have told you that you are off your rocker. Here I am though, and I thoroughly enjoyed it. It's certainly not the same as meeting and connecting in person but it serves its purpose while this virus rampages across our world. Today on the meeting, we talked about our character defects. The flaws of our character, that we have allowed to pile up without taking any responsibility for them. These shortcomings are what give us mental permission to silently suffer or take out our distresses on someone else. Always a great reminder, that we are never perfect and we are never done.

Daily, I go inward, where the only power to peace exists. I pray, I journal and give thanks to my higher power. If I would allow my character flaws of "my way or the highway" to dominate, I would not find peace. Awareness of this is liberating. I desire to this day, to work hard to be the person that my higher power would want for me. Take inventory, have faith and serve others. I attempt to do this in my life. I don't do it perfectly. That is why recovery is a process, not an event.

Something else I am noticing, is that I had become accustomed to the connection and gratitude from my recovery community, who I didn't see now other than on a screen or speaking with on the phone. My husband, although loving, didn't provide much of that. I had to search within myself the truth behind this awareness. My insight discovered that I have spent a lifetime helping others and talking with others and being of service, and I wasn't really doing much of that at all, quarantined to my home. So, I decided to get out my list of people I knew in recovery. I would attempt to reach out and call about three to four people every day, to check in with them, assist in any way I could, and connect. Being locked down at home, it seemed to me connecting with the outside world was important. Some I would just get answering machines, some it was a short chat and others it was a heartfelt discussion. This felt good to me.

The warmer weather has brought a welcomed patio season. Cathy has been driving down from Listowel to assist with our front terrace. She loves helping out with tasks like this and does it so well.

Cathy, a sensitive person by nature, noticed and quietly said with concern to me, that she thought Dave was off, even perhaps depressed. I hadn't noticed to be honest. He is not a chatty man. He has always been quieter by nature and he didn't say very much, very often. In the past, he wouldn't say too much to me as I continually shared my thoughts and feelings with him about life and occasionally, when I got to be too much, he would say enough is enough. Some noticed he was confused at times. I didn't think anything of his confusion, he was 90 after all and so the fact that he didn't remember things, was not a surprise to me. Traditionally, he didn't pay attention to what we were talking about most of the time and we would just laugh about it. If Dave wasn't interested or people were babbling on about nothing, he just tuned them out. So that fact that he wasn't keeping up with conversations, was his norm. It would be different if I was not connecting with others, listening attentively and responding, or forgetting bits of conversations. People would notice and think what the heck is wrong with Bev? But Dave was different than I. He was quiet, he was less engaged and I didn't think too much about it.

The medical and science community eventually starting talking about the affects of lockdown, especially in the senior community and the need for connection to avoid the isolation side affects. I guess it was helpful for me to do what I was doing and staying connected to folks through calls and through my iPad. Dave was not doing that nor would it be something he would ever do.

In lockdown for Dave's 90th birthday, our children and grandchildren planned a drive-by, socially distanced party. Dave and I stood at the top of the drive way while family and friends drove by and honked. Many parked and stood on the road, staying away from one and another, shouting out well wishes and dropping cards and gifts on the end of the driveway. Not what would have been planned otherwise, but none the less, a welcomed and lovely celebration.

Dave continued to show increasing signs of what I guess was depression during the isolation periods. A little more confusion was noticed, but I assumed that was a side affect of this isolation-depression.

It's fall now. Dave has been to his family doctor and it looks like he most likely has some dementia, which the doctor thought was mostly apart of being 90 years old. His symptoms are a little more pronounced now; more confusion, a little more emotion. He seems to get obsessive in thoughts and worries at times. The doctor has stated the progression of it, given the signs showing so late in the game will most likely be slow, but one never knows.

I just spoke and shared my experiences with folks at an online meeting for a friend's birthday of sobriety. I have known this friend for decades now. She is in her early 70s and has struggled with staying sober. Her struggles have spanned over decades and although she would try, she would have little or no long-term success. She jokes that she asked me to speak as she would have as many years of sobriety as I have had, if she had just done as I did. A lovely woman, with grown children and a supportive second husband; probably too supportive given her in and out of recovery. She has met many people through the years, many of which have attempted to help her.

I don't prepare what I am going to speak about at these birthday celebration meetings. I pray, I have quiet time. I sometimes think I should talk about this or that. Sometimes I remember to and sometimes I don't. Interestingly enough, this time when I spoke, I shared a story of something that I have never shared in the 49 years of doing speaking at meetings and I have spoke hundreds of times.

Sharing with the online audience, I was talking about how our program was not religious, and I wasn't trying to impose religion on anyone but that my early years of faith, as a small child, had a significant influence on me. I continued to articulate the memory of my great-grandfathers death and my great-grandmother sitting at his casket which was in their living room, as they did in those days, and her being blissfully at peace. She was okay with whatever was going on and said to me, "God has just called him ahead, Bevy. I will just wait until God calls me and we will be together again.". I shared with this group, that I wasn't trying to impose my beliefs but it was that kind of faith that helped me in good stead and I have been searching and trying to attain that kind of conviction, that amount of quiet and peace from that belief, ever since. When I had stumbled so far away from this way, I was filled with pain, remorse, shame and guilt. When I got sober, it took me back to the place that I had been searching for, all of those years.

Dave had told me that he was comfortable with me talking about his health and illness. So, I shared with this group (they all know Dave), that while it is a sad time to see these changes in my husband, that he has given to me and supported me, for all these years and now this recovery program was allowing me to have a good attitude and a sense of well-being, and be able to give back and support him now.

That is the power of spiritual living.

Dave went to the doctors for another check-up. He goes regularly for check-ups due to his past cancer diagnosis, to make sure all is well. Driving himself there, as he has dozens of times before, he returned home in a confused state. On his way to the appointment, he got lost.

His occasional confusion and forgetfulness have taken on a new dimension. His behaviors changing, his thoughts more obsessive about Covid or garbage pickup or whatever is consuming his mind in the moment. His emotions heightened. He is acting out more, sometimes angry eruptions. Being the only one around, often directed at me.

I am reminded, that rather than being selfish, impatient, unkind or any other feelings that go along with being frustrated or when seeking answers to something out of our control, such as a pandemic or the failing health of a loved one, to be patient. It is now I need to remind myself, that patience and tolerance is our code in spiritual living. I didn't always have this ability and some days I am prodded to practice harder. But without a doubt, my spirituality has allowed me to seek ways, spiritual ways to behave. I can accept the present reality from a spiritual point of view or a spiritual way of living. I pray daily and connect with my higher power. In doing so, I am much more tolerant and patient, which in the depths of my personality, doesn't come naturally to me and to this day, I still have to keep it in check.

My husband's health and being isolated alone together during this pandemic are obviously not ideal, but rather intense and difficult at times. But I trust that I can handle whatever it is that I, and we, experience. I give full credit to my spirituality, for it has schooled and prepared to assist me, to deal with my Davey's declining well-being. It allows me compassion; far more compassion than I ever thought I was capable of. If I am to be honest, the only thing I think of mostly, is it will be a sad day, if there is ever a day, when he doesn't remember us any longer.

The awareness of the reality of my relationship with my husband has also been on the forefront of my mind. I've had a pretty darn good life for a long time. Dave has been more than there for me. He has supported me though my darkest days and through my brightest moments. It hasn't been from afar either. Actively involving himself, Dave was a part of every corner of my life, volunteering at Westover and St. Stephens up until the last couple of years. As much a part of any of my successes, he has been a constant, quiet and gentle player, willingly standing in the shadows, without any accolades or awards.

When David video-calls us, he has such a way with his fun nature and his contagious smile and laugh. David could charm the birds out of the trees. The compassion and kindness towards his father is abundant. He knows what to say and how to say it, to make Dave smile or laugh. It makes everything perfect in the moment.

The world has changed. We have gotten far off track. The pandemic has perpetuated much. Lack of real connection and spiritual living has been replaced with materialistic possessions, instant superficial connection and appearances. It was present already but now while isolated in our homes, the intensity seems more obvious. We have gradually moved to the kind of world where we are displaced from deeper connections and where status and money have become our God. Everyone has two to three cars, a half-million-dollar home and flying to Greece for vacation.

When I was young during the war, we did acts of kindness to assist other people. After the war, more money was to be made and was available. When you went shopping, you paid for it with this money. It would be an oddity that people owed money to another. Then, along came credit and credit cards and people began to buy whatever and whenever they wanted to buy. Buy now, pay later. Instant gratification.

Even in my early adulthood, there was very little debt one would incur. Now, it is commonplace to be owing thousands of dollars to banks and credit companies. It has mushroomed. Everyone has these fancy cars and what was once rare is now mundane and custom. But no one has earned and paid for these possessions. Our concern for what is on sale and what we can consume as the consumer has replaced our concern for one and another. Everyone trying to out do each other and keep up with *the Jones.* More. More possessions, more debt.

This pandemic is almost forcing everyone to face the reality of their lives and truly see what is important. To connect with their spirits and to connect with each other. It is a time when perhaps some will see the necessity of conversion, from materialistic living to spiritual living.

When I was a kid, everyone went to church. Everyone. Now, the church is becoming a thing of yesterday and I get it. But it was a place where an individual could find spirituality or perhaps simply believe in something greater than themselves. Where are people finding their spirituality today? The rise of addiction, the rise of mental health disease, the rise of trauma, the rise of divorce, the rise of suicide, why? Could it be that it is the rise of soul-sickness? A generation and population, more void of spiritual living?

I feel some anxiousness now with the change in my husband's personality and his frequent chatter of his worries or obsessive thoughts. This accompanied with the lockdown, creates challenges.

There has been some lifting of the societal pandemic restrictions for now. We can gather in small circles. Dave is unable to drive now and well, I don't like to drive much farther than a store nearby, so my grandson Mathew and his new wife Joelle, have volunteered to come pick us up and take us for Thanksgiving dinner in Listowel with my son Rick and his other boys. I am excited to do so. Dave, on the other hand is not and got quite upset and even angry about the idea, for whatever reasoning his mind was offering him. So, we cancelled and I simply explained to family that he is not feeling up to it.

Dave and I have always lived very independent lives. He used to travel a lot for his work, while I was off bopping around from here to there and back again. I wasn't a typical housewife for my era. I never did his laundry or packed his bags when he travelled. I liked a nice home but I didn't care much for housecleaning, and that's why we have had a housecleaner for many years. I was accustomed to do what I wanted to do, when I wanted and he has bolstered me, every step of the way.

Now, I am being asked to be of service to him more. I feel fortunate to have the physical health and the acute mind that I do, to do so. I know that I would be dealing differently with life in this moment without my spiritual program. I make it a point to be aware of this. To remember that I would have dealt with the challenges I am faced with now, much more antagonistically without this way of life. I also remember as from time to time, I can still have thoughts and feelings of judgement, criticization and low-tolerance towards others. This awareness is liberating. It is through this inward acknowledgment, that I do what I need to do, to shift more into peace. Living the way I practice, allows me to not go into a tailspin with every adverse event.

The reality of this moment, is that I stay indoors and away from others to keep myself and others safe and we have limited visitors, a "bubble" as they are calling it.

When Dave yells at me, in his confused state, it doesn't upset me or bother me too much but it does require me to adjust to this new personality and the changes that have come along with his condition.

I am attempting to continue to be as honest as I can be about the realism of today. We seek and listen to medical advice, get the support and treatment that he and we need and be honest about the expected progression. Sad as it is, I can also stay in the reality, be there for him and feel blessed for the life we have had. I have had pretty good for a long, long time.

That's what living a spiritual life has offered me. That's what my spiritual program has given me.

Having relief, with visits from others, is important to us now. David with direction from his husband Clive, is insisting anyone that comes to visit us, gets tested prior. My oldest Rick does just that and comes by to assist, taking Dave for a drive in the car or anything else he can do. Rick says he will be doing for us whatever we need done, as he hasn't forgotten those endless trips that Dave would drive me to go see him and his sister, week after week after week. Brenda, Rick's ex-wife would often say that Dave was the only grandfather that her kids ever had, attending every grandchild's sporting event for decades. She would say that the kids had her dad and D.R. but they were not actively present in the same way, that Grandpa Dave was. She has been very good to me and really embraced and included me in all family functions which was so appreciated.

Dave has quietly been in the background during our life together, being an exceptional man. So, the fact that he is yapping away now, in his demented state, of his obsession about the weather or the pandemic, doesn't matter. He can't help what his brain is telling him now. Under his illness, he is simply the reserved, dear soul that I know he is.

My niece and God-daughter Kelly and my sister Anne, get their Covid-19 tests and come visit every week or two. Dave seems to like to have something to look forward to when he knows that people will be coming for lunch or a visit. Kelly is teaching him some mindfulness and breathing techniques. Dave is receptive to learn and does so. However, I am not sure if they are helping Dave, as he fell asleep while doing them.

My dear friends Val and Kevin, also taking precautions and visit often. Dave really loves going for drives in the country with Kevin. They are both such a welcomed support and avenue of love, to both Dave and I.

Despite the hopes of a slow progression of Dave's dementia, it doesn't appear to be the case. The doctor has referred us to the dementia assessment care, we have been through the triage, and they let us know that would be a couple of months perhaps. He is becoming more irrational and agitated on some days more than others and he is not sleeping well, often waking me up in the middle of the night, with concern to get the garbage out or something like that.

Kelly and Val, are both nurses. I lean on them from time to time for medical input. Kelly feels that that perhaps things have progressed quicker than expected and is concerned about the progression of his emotional outbreaks and suggests we should call the doctor or the triage to let them know. She had worked on an Alzheimer and dementia floor before and is worried about his agitation and confusion, turning to lashing out to me or harm to himself. I agree and plan to reach out to the doctor's offices.

My niece shares with me that she is going away to her friends this weekend. Her friend had purchased an old retreat centre owned by the Catholic church down in Port Burwell. Ironically, it is the very same Catholic retreat centre that I had attended in 1985 when Sister St. Patrick told me to go there and surrender while we waited for funding for Westover.

The cleaning lady from my usually cleaning service company is off and they sent a new lady. When I opened the door to invite her in, I immediately noticed her friendly nature as well as the coat she was wearing. The coat had a large emblem on it that said *Westover Treatment Centre.* I told her I liked her coat and the enthusiasm spilled from her voice as she shared about the centre and how it saved her life. Her excitement amplified when I told her who I was.

The synchronicities of coincidence always amuse me.

Today, I masked-up for protection and went out to the store by myself. I don't feel overly worn-out by it all, but I do think that it is good for me get out from the four-walls of confinement in my home, and be on my own. Respite from the home given the reality of state of mind my dear husband is in, I think, is okay.

Dave was finally going for his dementia appointment at Parkwood. He knew about the appointment and was quite agreeable to go. However, on the way to the appointment, he became unsettled and cantankerous, angrily yelling "what the hell do we have to do this for?"

Christmas is approaching, Dave's condition has drastically declined and we are back in a lockdown with small bubble parameters. Given the current facts of existence, I have decided it best we not go anywhere. Val and Kevin are in London and one of them visit almost daily. Family comes frequently as well. My children are encouraging me to consider moving from London, closer to them in Listowel. David, although living in the U.K. agrees.

Poor Dave is now more troubled than not. The medical folks have discussed that perhaps the dementia has affected the parts of his brain that control emotion. I don't think I have heard my husband raise his voice, let alone cuss in our life together. Now, yelling profanities and screaming out has become an every day occurrence. Dave often has episodes where he has hands begin to shake. He says he feels it coming. "Here we go again" and he will try and get up to go lay on his bed. Once lying down, he thrashes about, throwing pillows and blankets, shaking uncontrollably and yelling "babababababa" over and over. He says "Baba" takes over him, "he's in my brain."

Certainly, sad to see a quiet, gentle man such as Dave, change and struggle as he is. I don't take it personally; I know its his disease.

Kevin is staying overnight, every night now. It is felt that it is needed for my safety, as well as poor Davey's.

So, I planned a quiet Christmas with Kevin, Dave and I but unfortunately Dave had an unusually difficult day and we tended to him for most of the day. Our Christmas dinner consisted of some mashed potatoes, late in the evening.

Anne and Kelly, brought us leftovers on Boxing Day from their Christmas. Dave worries a lot about choking on his food so we had some soup and other soft items. Despite this being a better day for him, his decline was evident to them.

David, concerned with the weakening and deterioration of this father, and books a flight home to Canada. Upon his arrival in Toronto, he shows address proof where he will isolate for two weeks. My sister's other daughter Tracey lives in Hong Kong but still has a home in Oakville. David holes up there alone in their house for the fourteen days of quarantine. He is fortunate with his job at the Cardiff University, that he can work remotely. His sister Cathy takes him some food, which he thought was a perfect time to do a cleanse. She delivers him bags of lemon, cayenne pepper and maple syrup for his annual New Years food purge to reset his system.

The two weeks are up and Kelly picks him up to bring him home to us. These two are peas in a pod and always enjoy each others company. David has a blunt awakening to the reality of his father's condition as they step through our front door and Dave is having one of his yelling "bababa" moments. Without hesitation, David goes to his father, holds his hand and begins to soothe him.

This was the way it was; the entire time David was here. No one, I mean no one could soothe Dave, like his son could. His way, his words, his guidance to take deep breaths, whatever it was, Dave responded to David in such a way. As difficult as the situation was, that was a beautiful thing to witness.

We finally got Dave into the hospital for some help and medication. We were hopeful the medication would provide him some ease. Due to the lockdown and strict visiting rules there, only one of us could visit a day. Unfortunately, visitors would gown and mask up and whether it was me, Val, Kevin or one of the kids, Dave would often just tell whoever to get out and go home. The only person that seemed to be able to sit for any length of time with him on a visit was Rick, as Rick would come prepared with a list of things to discuss and focus on, such as sport stats and game results. Dave enjoyed talking about that.

The plan was to get him into Braemer Nursing home for now, which was a half hour or so from Listowel. The wheels were also in motion for me to put the house up for sale, and move to Listowel as well. Fortunately, my grandson Brandon was a top-notch real estate agent, my daughter Cathy an extraordinary organizer and multi-tasker and my son David, home to assist and organize it all.

The cyclonic whirlwind of how fast everything was happening made me spin. Cathy and David were focused and on task, cleaning out a life time of junk in the basement, organizing the downsize of furniture and fixtures, from the two-level, multi-room condo we resided in, to the one bedroom and one room apartment they had found for me at the Maitland Terrace retirement community home in Listowel.

In the midst of this chaos, they found David a bed near Listowel at Braemer home.

Kevin, David and I packed some belongings and our dear Dave into the car for the journey to his new home.

It was an awful winter day. We drove slowly due the gusts of blowing snow. When we arrived at the home, they had informed us of their very strict Covid-19 rules, obviously due the nature of their residence. They told us to go around to the side door and that we would not be able to go in the building as they had a strict no visitor policy.

Dave, seemingly aware of what was about to happen, got very quiet. He seemed mostly concerned about what would happen to his "sweetie" and how I would get along, meanwhile he was the one being displaced and experiencing a terminal disease. There is no point in pretending it wasn't what it was.

We drove around to where they instructed us and waited. Kevin and I were useless and crying. It's not that I lost peace or faith, but I think simply experiencing normal feelings and emotions, given the situation.

They opened the door and David got out of the car, the snow blowing and blistering, all around him. They greeted him in the full personal protection equipment and handed him some papers to sign. They were DNR (do not resuscitate) papers and so on. Once the papers were signed, David came to fetch his father to assist him to the building door. As confused as his state may have been, he seemed to know exactly what was happening. My dear husband began to cry uncontrollably, grabbing and hanging on to anything he could in the car to anchor himself while begging us, "no, no, no".

David, had to grab and assist his father almost forcibly to exit the vehicle and hand him over to the caregivers at the nursing home. There they were, snow blasting aggressively against them, a caregiver on each side of my poor Davey's arms, as he was looking back, wildly and desperately sobbing and pleading with us to not leave him. It was bluntly, a nightmare.

They took him inside, the door shut and Kevin, David and I sat in the car and wept for some time. Without a single doubt, this is easily the worst day of my life.

David had planned to stay for a month but ended up staying for about three. My grandson, Brandon easily sold our home within days or so it seemed. Cathy had painted and measured my new apartment that I was to be moving into, so we knew what furniture would fit in it. Much of my material belongings were auctioned off so speak, for free to whatever family wanted them. That which they didn't, I donated to St. Stephens, or Turning Point (a home for women that Val was running) or gave to a charity.

Poor Dave had to be quarantined with no visitors and no socialization of others at the home for fourteen days, if you can imagine. Not home, in new place, alone other than masked and gowned strangers/ staff going in and out from time to time. He became more aggressive, more confused and then violent. This was a total contradiction to anything he ever was.

As the kids helped me rearrange and organize, I didn't really have time to process much. I finally cracked one day and just sobbed. Within a matter of a few months, my life had been turned completely upside down and I was not doing the things I know I should be doing. So, I allowed myself to feel, I prayed, I reached out to people in my fellowship, and went within to find peace. Shortly after doing what I needed to do, my spiritual connection re-ignited more strongly to my higher power. I found my trust and knowing, that no matter what happens, I will be okay.

      I recollected how I had tried to be stern and I tried to be compassionate with Dave to see if it would have helped. It did not. I understand he was incapable of anything else. The doctors, the nurses and my spiritual program helped me to understand what is, as it is and so, it is. I prayed. I prayed for him and us. I let go of the guilt I felt from any ways I minimized his illness initially, or spoke to him in haste, understanding this was his illness.

      After Dave's quarantine time was over, we had hoped the socialization would outweigh any effects of being isolated. Cathy would take him pizza and beer on Friday nights, as that was a thing he enjoyed when he was living at home. Unfortunately, the behavior became too disruptive for the nursing home and they were not equipped for it. They were transferring him to Stratford

Hospital, which was about 40 minutes from Listowel and just under an hour from London.

As my belongings became boxes, and my furniture donned labels of their final destinations, Dave ended up in a bed in the hospital and under the care of the psychiatry department. He was allowed one visitor a day and we made a list and schedule for who would be there on what day. Not a day went by from that day forward, without someone that loved him connecting with him in person.

At the hospital, they medicated him with some psychotropic medication; antipsychotics and mood stabilizers and he responded positively to them. The episodes decreased and he was generally content for the most part.

Dave's medication gave him the reprieve from his illness that allowed his son to have a meaningful conversation. David was able to tell his father how much he meant to him, how appreciative he was of his unconditional love and support and how much he loved him. It allowed me to say all of what I wanted to say to my beloved husband, as well.

David has been here for three months now, was to go back to Wales, to his husband and his home. His work has been most generous with letting him work very minimal hours remotely from Canada.

We said our good-byes to David as he returned home to Wales, knowing that the next time he would be home would most likely be a celebration of his father's life. We had honest conversations, knowing that his father was 90 years old and he was not going to recover from this.

David left London to the airport with his cousin Kelly, commenting on the sharp emotion he was experiencing. He was grateful to have had the opportunity to see his father clearer minded and to share that connection and conversation that he had with his dad, but also knowing he mostly likely wouldn't see him alive again. He also noted some poignancy of knowing that his mother was moving and when he returned "home" again, it would not be to London, Ontario which had been his home and his home to return to, his entire life.

One day, when exiting Dave's hospital room, (probably because he told me I could go now, as he did often shortly after I arrived), I noticed on the big staff board by Dave's name that his doctor and psychiatrist's name was Dr. Judson. I asked the nurse if she knew what the doctors first name was. She informed me she did not, but it wouldn't take her much to find out and she would get back to me. I thought it interesting, that Dave's doctors name was the same as my good friend in the addiction field, Dr. Judson.

Then just like that, Dr. Judson, the psychiatrist entered the hallway. I asked him if he was Dave's doctor and he confirmed. I asked him if his father was Dr. Judson from London. He also confirmed. I asked if by chance he remembered me but he was unsure. Fact is, we had actually met before when his father introduced him to me at a recovery meeting. When I reminded him, he absolutely remembered who I was, beneath my protective mask, that we all were wearing everywhere. He is kind and spoke thoughtfully, just as his father does.

The man taking care of my Davey now, is a blanket of comfort and familiarity.

I have the home in London for another month or so, to arrange for the rest of our items to be removed, donated or stored, but I have been officially living in Listowel now for ten days. I have this lovely apartment and if I am to be honest, it is small. I have lived in larger homes most of my life and this was going to take a little getting used to.

It is Dave's 91st birthday. He is on the main floor at the Stratford hospital. His medication doesn't seem to have the same effect it did initially but it certainly was helping him on some levels.

We had arranged for family to come to stand outside the hospital window for his birthday, in shifts. The pandemic restrictions still only allow one person to visit per day. I stayed in his room with him and Rick, my grandson Christopher, our great-grandson Cohen, Matthew, Anne and Kelly came early. Cathy and her gang were coming later.

Dave got up in the chair facing the window and the first crew arrived. We could hear the muffled voices on the other side of the window as I sat in the room with Dave, with our family had their faces pressed up close, waving and well-wishing. It was a blessing that Dave recognized every single family that came to the window that day. He asked about his other great grandson and his namesake Davis, who was just a toddler and not present. He understood whatever everyone was saying, he laughed and happy cried. He read a birthday card from a family friend, Kyle McKenzie. Then he looked at Mathew and held up two fingers. No one knew, but Mathew and Joelle had told me that they were expecting twins and that I could share that with Dave. Dave was so happy as he looked at Matt, holding up his two fingers and no one knowing what was going on but the two of them.

He barely remembered anything or anyone, anymore. That day, and in that moment, he remembered everyone and everything.

It was a blessed day.

After we waved and blew kisses to everyone, and everyone walked away from that hospital window, Dave contently looked at me and said, "you can go now sweetie".

I couldn't believe the clarity he had that day, after weeks and months of foggy confusion. I shared this experience with my friend Dr. Judson Sr. He told me not to try and rationalize it and to not try and figure it out, but to know that it was a day of grace. "That is one explanation, that medicine can not explain", he told me.

So, I accepted. A day of grace.

For that, I am deeply grateful.

But the challenges were not over. Stratford was having a surge of Covid19 patients and needed Dave's bed. I had just moved from London to be closer to my husband 13 days ago. Two days after our day of grace we had received the news they were transferring Dave to Parkwood Hospital, in London. There was a new unit at Parkwood, bringing in medical people from all departments for advanced or end stage dementia patients, so I packed up and stayed with Val.

My Davey was transferred to Parkwood. His appetite had been diminishing for sometime now but once settled into the new home back in the city of our old home, his strength and will to continue, was over. He was no longer eating.

Parkwood had similar pandemic restrictions as the rest but with our numerous requests, they made some provisions for visitors given his failing state. Kevin went out and got us a new iPad so that David could visit with his father from Wales. Staff was very kind and helpful to assist. Despite Dave being incapable of really communicating any more, a new age virtual connection could still happen for my son and my husband.

The Pastor was a lovely woman, informing us she would be available for us whenever needed. Over the next two days, I sat by his bed side, along with my children Cathy and Rick in person, David virtually and Val and Kevin too. We would talk to him but he was saying very little, if anything. No more cursing, no more yelling, no belligerent out of character behavior. He was fading.

Despite his inability to respond with any sort of substantiation, I held his hand and talked to him. I told him everything I should have been saying for sixty years. I told him how wonderfully supportive he was to me, no matter where I was going or what I was doing. His love, was a true unconditional love and I let him know how deeply grateful I am for our life together.

Val came to visit. We were sitting at his hospital bedside talking and talking, as we do. Dave's breathing was laboured. There was no flailing. He simply appeared peaceful, laying comfortable.

We stepped out of the room for a minute for staff care and when we came back into the room he was no longer breathing. It was okay, expected and I had prayed for this. It was my answer. It was so quiet in the room with his own quietness. He was calm again. Calm is who he always was.

We didn't wait for the doctor to pronounce him. There was nothing there left for us to stay for. I didn't shed any tears as this was an answer.

He was now at peace, and I was at peace too.

Over the next few days, after getting family and friends informed, I needed to take time for myself to process. I surrendered more to my higher power, I amped up my practice of praying and with that always felt a presence of my God, of my understanding. This brought me to a place of quiet acceptance, peace and ease.

As the weeks progressed and time went on, I had no choice but to face the reality of my life now. I was living alone, something I had never done before. I often feel aloneness, emptiness and sadness in this new life without my Davey. I had been spending months looking after of him. Truly through our decades together, there was nothing but support. I miss him dearly.

There is a void and I feel sadness but I am okay. I certainly miss my London community and friends. I often wonder. if I wasn't so caught up in the whirl of me and my husbands emotional state and if I had been more of my aligned self, if I would have resisted moving right away. When their father began to fail, our children's wheels were in hyper-motion to sell, pack and move. It is a lot to process. I have such amazing family support and attention at levels I couldn't imagine. However, sometimes sitting in my small apartment, without the comfort of the home I was used to, nor all my friends I connected to daily and with the absence of my partner in life, I feel a little lost.

It is important for me to concentrate on processing and getting my spirit caught up to speed with the many reasons and there are many, of why it was a good move for me.

The fact that I was not talking and validating how I was feeling, is a contradiction of what I have been yammering about for all these years. I am not a complainer so I didn't want to be complaining. It is not that I wasn't grateful for all that I had, there was just a big piece missing. So as to not complain or not seem ungrateful I pushed away any emotions contradicting this. More each day, I started to identify with what is going on with me- discussing and processing and assimilating.

I often thought, "what is next for me?" Dave is gone, I have moved to another town, I don't have all my groups and meetings, I don't have my community around me, what is my purpose at 88 years old?

I had to remember and make sure that I continue to be needed, and wanted and loved. My soul needed that. I needed to connect with other people's souls. Don't get me wrong, every relationship doesn't have to have deep and powerful conversations. Life would be monotonous and exhausting if so. I love a silly chit chat and good laugh, but right now, my soul craved deeper connection. To remedy this, I stay very connected with my family, friends and spiritual program. I find great purpose with talking to others that are new to the program, those suffering individuals needing connection, as they try and save their soul.

My new apartment building had lots of action on the daily. While asked to play bridge a lot, it took me a bit to know what I wanted and what I didn't. So, I gave myself permission to create space to heal, to mourn, to adjust and to connect with my soul desires.

Each morning, I continued to wake up, pray and meditate and do some spiritual reading. I often started out with a flat feeling and it only would take a call from someone in need or a deeper level conversation for me to understand and connect to my purpose. My personality needs people and my soul needs to be of service.

More and more, if I stay living a spiritual existence, I am okay where I am because my spiritual life allows me to have great peace, wherever I am plunked. I will be 89 years old soon. I have no fear of death, while still enjoying life gratefully as it evolves, until it is time.

I am grateful to know this. Many will quit whatever behavior that created chaos in their life without filling the soul and without this deeper spiritual relationship. They may not be acting in chaotic destructive ways but their soul remains bankrupt and unfulfilled.

Deep, deep connection is required for a soul connection. I know I am here for a spiritual purpose and supporting my purpose, guides me to a better place.

I am learning to be comfortable on my own. I have my family and am blessed to be so close with my children and to be able to watch my great grandchild's hockey games.

I have trust and a knowing that I will be just fine. I still feel dull some days but also feel grateful and the two can coexist together. That is important to remember. Opposing emotions can coexist. Its not this or that.

I continue to still be searching and seeking my next adventure.

As coronavirus rampages on, I am learning that every day spiritual living must include this global viral pandemic. I was becoming more opinionated, less patient and generally crazy. My ego had me convinced that if someone didn't see my point of view, they've got to be nuts. I haven't been this obsessed in years.

I had become fixated on the external and unhappy with those that were not thinking like me. I wasn't off base with trusting doctors and so on but I was sounding off and not feeling like I was simply presenting my position but rather judging and trying to prove that my point was right.

This is what is referred to as a spiritual blackout. Generally speaking, I can catch my arrogant and judgmental thinking in a flash. But today, my spiritual arrogance was winning.

Normally, I was accepting of all no matter how goofy or crazy they might be in this moment, without judgment. But currently, I was allowing others' opinions and actions to affect my thoughts, feelings and connection to my soul. And when that is happening, its me that is the goofy, crazy one.

This was causing me to become increased restless and disturbed. I didn't recognize this right away. Finally, I thought "never mind others' opinions, covid and freedom rallies, what about Bev?"

It was time to reset in a spiritual time out.

I knew I needed to focus more on what I want, rather that what I didn't. I knew I needed to focus on internal rather than external fixations. After 50 years of spiritual recovery, I knew I needed to turn it over to my higher power, trust, take inventory and quit blaming external situations for causing me restlessness and lack of ease. It is important to continue mindful conscious thinking so I don't get pulled back or influenced by the outside external or other people. To move forward and return to a place of inner peace at all costs, I had to follow my program, get out of my head and into my heart.

You simply can not intellectualize spirituality.

I miss my Dave in the mornings, as he brought me a coffee in bed each day. That daily connection we had for decades was gone. I feel alone until I reconnect with myself. I continue to give myself permission to feel sad and miss him. I reflect on him and our sweet memories.

I continue my daily practice starting with inspirational (in-spirit) reading, praying and meditating.

"God, I offer myself to Thee to build with me & to do with me as Thou wilt. Relieve me of the bondage of self, that I may better do Thy will. Take away my difficulties, that victory over them may bear witness to those I would help of Thy Power, Thy love & Thy way of life. May I do Thy will always."

At the end of the day, I take inventory, journal any insights or revelations and always practice gratitude. In between the start and end of the day, I do what I can to connect and be in service.

This keeps me aligned and my soul full.

I often wonder if this chapter has me quieter and more satisfied with ample free time. This certainly doesn't seem like my nature. Perhaps it is speaking and sharing more or pursuing something else? I will continue to follow my guidance from my soul and my higher power. I put this question out wondering if and when the answer will expose itself to what I am suppose to be doing with my time. Where do I fit in?

Although I have an ongoing trust that the answers will be revealed to me from my higher power, what I am learning is that I need to be talking about it with like-minded friends.

So, I have begun just that. I talked to my friend Kevin about all this. Ironically, he said "Someone who has committed to a life as full and interesting as yours, you need to write a book about your life. If you are still seeking to learn and grow at your age, you need to share that with the world." It is true that many don't do the work as my friend is suggesting I have. "5% of the people only do 90% of the work required."

Kevin reminded me this is an example of growing and evolving continuously for all of our life, and that some folks, when they start a spiritual recovery within a year, they think they know it all. To which we laughed and I said "at one year in, I thought I did too!".

A few months have passed. I have found a spiritual recovery meeting here in my new hometown. I play bridge, I go to chair yoga, and I am the new Chair of the Residents Association of my retirement home.

I am deeply grateful that my friends from London come and see me often. Each week, people are driving back and forth to visit. We often go for lunch at the local golf course. Sometimes, they just come and pick me and take me back to London for a few days for meetings and luncheons and so on. This is no ten-minute drive either, but an hour and half.

My children are nearby always. David and I zoom chat weekly. Cathy is always mindful to pick me up or pick something up for me at the stores when she goes. Rick is often chauffeuring me to go out and see my great-grandsons sporting events of the day. He or my grandson Christopher will pick me up each time. On Sundays, we often gather at Brenda's for dinner with all the grandkids and great grandkids. Brenda and Rick, although not together as a couple continue to recognize family with no need for their children to run around splitting their time for family occasions. This is just lovely to witness for everyone. Rick and Brenda's amicability brings a delightful chaos for Sunday dinners with their 3 boys, their lovely wives and 5 young, loud and sometimes wild children. I just simply love it all.

I don't have a chance to feel lonely and my appreciation for the continued connections fills my cup. However, I still am deeply grieving and missing my sweetheart.

Dave didn't do all this running around for me but he was always just quietly sitting there stoically, with his hands folded. I often visualize and feel him doing just that, for whatever reason usually on the weekends. I feel him just sitting there on a chair watching all this performance of my new existence. Hands always resting in a folded way, like any picture of him depicts.

I don't want him back the way he was. I certainly don't feel his leaving cheated us of anything. We lived a wonderful and full life together. I simply miss him.

Despite all the activities and busyness that has re-developed in my life, I feel quieter within. My spirituality keeps me in touch with my peace which is imperative. I feel connected now, more so than the final months of Dave's life.

My story most certainly has a new dimension to it when I speak which for whatever reason has been asked of me more frequently lately. This, like much of life now, is done virtually on Zoom as the pandemic restrictions are still in effect. It isn't the same as in person but it is something. Some folks only know virtual recovery as they arrived to it during the lockdowns.

Traditionally at meetings, when I share my soul sickness story, I shared about my drinking as a result of not being a good mother and the guilt and shame I felt. I had always articulated that it didn't matter what my ex-husband was doing or what my reason were but that I had left those small children behind and that this had created chaos in my soul. Of course, through the years, the story evolved when I discovered (through Dave) more awareness that drinking myself to death and being a lush of a mother was not the solution and finding a spiritual program and eventually developing a stronger relationship with my children again.

But now, people love hear the next chapter of this story; that the children that I had walked away from all those years ago are now the very children that have called me back to them. Now, instead of me looking after my children, they are looking after their mother. It has come full circle.

I am grateful for my life as a result of a spiritual life provided to me through my program and through the Grace of God. I am reminded again and again, even after decades of healing that many don't recognize their soul sickness. For me and many others, it was obvious when I was stone cold passed out from drinking my pain away.

Others have no problem quitting the drinking, gambling, shopping or whatever obsessive and compulsive ways of thinking and acting they had participated in, to fill their voids. However, these folks still have the hole, they still have the soul sickness and will continue to until they fill their souls with what the soul needs and not a temporary numbing.

Spirituality is a part of the holistic being and needs mindful attention just as the body and mind do. I often think that if we paid more attention to the spirit, the body and mind would probably not suffer as much as it can.

I am also reminded to keep it simple and despite years of living a spiritual practice, it will always be a practice and not a perfection. I continue to take inventory of myself (not others), trust in my higher power and serve others that are suffering, like many of us have.

When I feel disturbed, the answer to almost all my problems is acceptance. It could be that I have found a person, an opinion, a thing, a conversation or a situation to be unacceptable to me and this takes my peace away. When I feel this, all I must do is accept what is, as it is. I must accept life completely on life's terms or I can not be happy. I need to concentrate not so much on what needs to be changed in the world but more so, what needs to be changed within me.

This is an ongoing practice and like all things, gets easier with practice.

It is March 2023. I had just celebrated 52 years of sobriety and living a life in spiritual recovery. A man named Jim has invited me to speak on a panel at a provincial conference of spiritual recovery in Toronto. I would be a key note speaker on the "long-timers" panel. I have attended this conference several times and there are usually thousands and thousands of people that attend.

I mean this in no egotistical way but in recovery, people know the ones that have been around for awhile and many people knew me. When I first got sober in 1979 this spiritual recovery program had only been around for 40 something years, so not any had 50 plus years of sobriety. It was all the buzz if there was an old-timer in the room or to meet. There was respect for the "royalty of recovery" so to speak. Not that anyone was better than others, but so much respect was given for doing the work, showing others, being of service and giving back for so many years.

Whenever we headed out to hear a panel during this 3-day conference, I would get stopped in the hallways and talked to by many as everyone thought they knew me at this conference. Most didn't really, they just knew *of* me. My friends would joke that we needed to start out to these panels a couple of hours earlier just to get there in time as there was so much engagement with people on our conference hallway travels.

It was the Saturday of the conference and while getting ready to speak on my long-timers panel, I had a realization and recollection. 50 years prior, in the infancy of my sobriety, I spoke at this same conference on the "new-comers" panel for the first time. I remember my sponsor Geri and friend Bea came to support me and as I look back, I had made much fuss about being a speaker. I had been a nervous basket case here all those many years ago. I can't imagine what I said back then when I spoke but was acknowledged as an active, willing and grateful newcomer and did what I was asked to in regards to following the recovery program.

That was my first time speaking at a conference of this magnitude and I have probably spoken about 8 times in between. Today, I am here 50 years after the initial time and feel pleased and grateful to be asked back.

This conference is celebrating its 80th year. The first one at the Royal York in Toronto in 1943 had about 80 people attend. Now with thousands attending, I am about to share my story of recovery and how I have stayed spiritually healthy for the last half of century.

It's hard to sum up 90 years of life in the 25–30-minute window you are allotted to speak. So, I embrace my usual routine of always praying before I speak to be guided to say what my higher power would have me say. I do this every, single time before I speak or go to a meeting. Today was no different.

When I took the podium, I shared with the attendees the fun fact that it was 50 years ago when I first took to a stage at this very conference as a new-comer, with only a couple years of sobriety. I shared the story of my first drink. I was at a fancy cocktail party, in a lovely home, sipping on champagne from long-stem crystal glasses, served on silver trays. I want the newcomers to remember, this is my first drink. Then, I share my low point; sitting in a private public bathroom stall at the market, with one foot on the broken-hinged door to keep it shut, sucking on a bottle of cheap wine and alone.

A priest had pulled me aside years ago and shared he thought the reason people can associate with my story (and believe me, there are far more traumatic and horrible stories than mine), was because of the bathroom story; an identifiable low and private point and in a place where you are always by yourself.

I then shared with this group that there is no doubt in mind, that if I were to pick up a drink today, even champagne from a fancy flute, I would end up in a bathroom, alone and drinking in despair. It just simply would not take me years to hit bottom again. My drinking was a symptom of a deeper trouble, my emotional situation that created a hole in my soul. I must always remember this and never allow the calamity of addiction to supersede my serenity.

I try to give a message of hope and inspiration. I most often don't remember what all I say, and always mentioned, I am guided on what to say through prior prayer. I do know most were exceptionally fond of the fact that I had spoken on the newcomer panel five decades before by the responses given to me afterward. People say the talk made them feel good. I often think of Maya Angelos quote when folks say that to me. *"People will forget what you said, people will forget what you did but people will never forget how you made them feel."*

I was grateful for the opportunity to be there at the conference and to be asked to speak on this panel.

This summer, St. Stephens who is now run by our dear friend Kevin held their annual charity golf tournament. Many of my family and friends, including my sister, my son and grandson and cousins came out. Even my great-grandson played with his dad and grandpa Rick. Besides by son, grandsons and great-grandson's team winning the tournament, the highlight for me was that they changed the name of the tournament to the Dave Thomson Charity Golf Tournament in memory of my beloved. This made my heart burst with joy.

I am unsure what the rest of my days hold for me. I know I am blessed with loving people in my life. I know I will continue to live the principles of the spiritual program that saved my soul. I will remember my past not to wallow in all the horrible things and places that this dis-ease took me to, but to leave the door open to it just a little bit to remember. I will continue to share my story so that it can help others. That being said, in spite of the fact that I have been taught to not regret the past, I regret the fact that I was not with my children when they were younger, no matter what the reasons why or who was at fault for that. Nothing I am going to do or say, or anything my children could do or say, will change this regret.

I have a pretty clear understanding of how I need to live my life. I believe we all live by progress rather than perfection and anyone that thinks they have it perfected is most likely living in la-la-land. I believe I can accept others as they are, without being judgemental. I know the difference between recognizing how people are in this moment and can share with people this observation without it being judgemental but rather mindful and factual, on where they are at on their road and the way they are behaving. I was not put on this earth to decide who should be doing what. That also doesn't mean I need to surround myself with people that don't want to make change for whatever reasons to make themselves feel better, its not for me to judge or change. It's none of my business what others do.

If I am really grateful for what I have been given and what I believe to be a gift, then I am certainly not running around telling others how they should be living life or criticizing others because they are not behaving in a certain way, that I think they should be. That's a contradiction.

I am as accepting about myself and my life, as I can be. Perhaps if I live another year or few, maybe I will be even more so? Generally, I am also good at allowing everyone else to live their life as they choose, knowing that everyone is doing the best they can, in this moment, with the tools they have. I try not to give unwanted advice. Forcing my opinion on anyone is not of service to anyone, including me. I will continue to not give advice, but offer my experience, when asked.

I continue to internalize the values that I have gained through my spiritual recovery which has brought life-altering gifts. I have faith that no matter where I am at or whatever it is that I am doing in this world, that is exactly where I am suppose to be. I don't ever think I should be doing something else, with someone else other than what is. I honor what is, as it is and have a faith in that. I believe everything that has happened and what is happening in my life, is exactly as it should be because I turn my will and my life over to my higher power every day.

I don't always do everything right, in every hour of the day. I am human. But if I do honest, mindful and regular inventory of myself I can keep practicing and make changes. I look to my higher power to assist me to do this. Acceptance offers me the ability to admit to myself when I am wrong by noticing a feeling of discomfort or guilt. Then I take action and admit to the other when I am wrong, by moving from feeling discomfort to expressing action. I take responsibility of my words, thoughts and actions, I wished I had done differently. When I feel that I may have been at fault, I attempt to own it, make amends and keep practicing.

I am by nature an opinionated person. My opinions over many years have shifted from "if they would just listen to me, they would have it all figured out" to now just sharing my experience, my strength, my hope and allowing them to form their own opinions and then I let it go. What others do with the information and their life is entirely up to them. No one can force others, it must be done in divine time, not my time. Just because we give someone the information doesn't mean they will go on to live happily ever after. I learned that by just looking at my own past when I was told to make changes and how I should be living but was incapable of it at that point in my life.

When we focus on ourselves (and not others), when we take our inventory (and not others), when we pay more attention to our thoughts, feelings and actions (and not others), we shift from ego to spiritual awakening. This is how we live a life of peace and feel peace in our soul. Spirituality is living in the space and energy of love and ease.

I am 90 and who knows, maybe I will live as long as Aunt Paulie. She lived to 105 years old and was full of business until 103. I am peaceful and content. I love to make fun of myself and love when other people do the same. I will keep living the best I can. I trust the divine plan for me and I have a spiritually abundant and peaceful soul.

What more could I ask for?

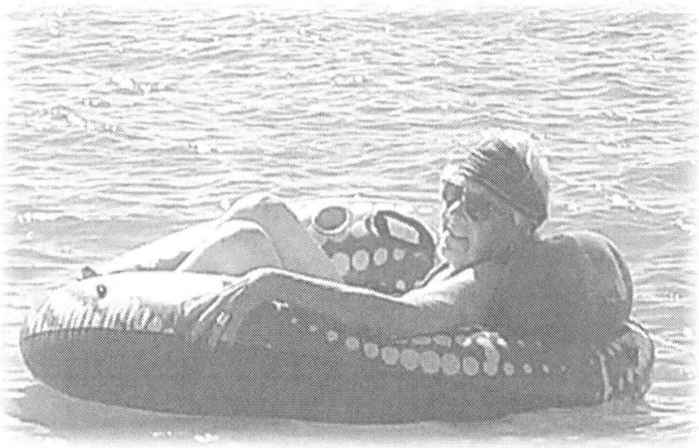

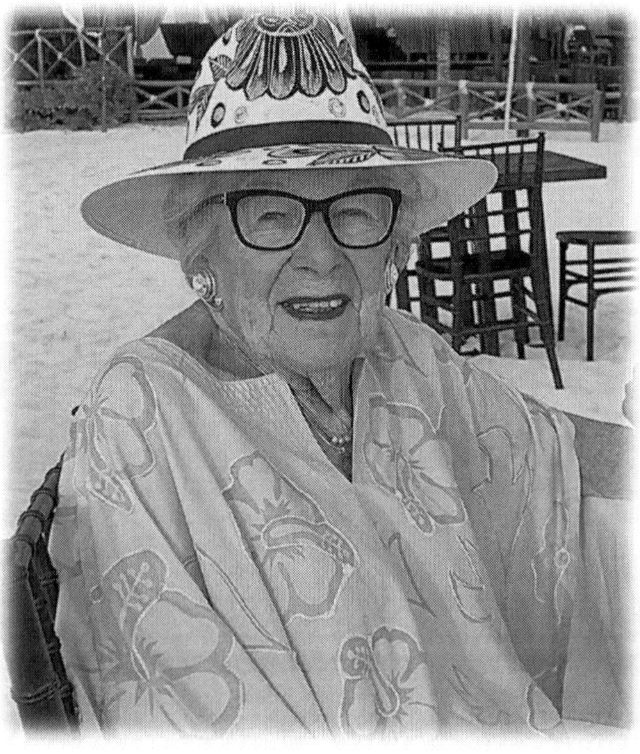

Epilogue

from the Author

When we are suffering, or when we are feeling more dis-ease or lack of ease than we feel peace, or when we feel difficulty and despair showing up in different areas in our life or repetitively over and over, we may be suffering from spiritual bankruptcy.

Past experiences or trauma may be still living rent-free in our souls. There is a commonality in spiritual disease. I personally think more and more people are afflicted by this today. We all are taught about (even if we don't always practice it) the importance of eating healthy and exercising for our bodies. In recent years we talk more about mental health and the need to take care of our minds.

But we don't hear a lot of spiritual talk, do we? Again, spirituality not being religion although you could find it through that avenue. But the deeper connection to something greater than us. No matter what religion or even atheist, spirituality is simply an adjective that is used to describe the search for one's place in the universe and our connection in it. It could be following the principles of mindfulness, non-judgmental acceptance, focusing on yourself rather than others, it could be seeking peace as the primary goal. Higher power could mean God but it could also mean Mother Earth or a connection to nature or to all human beings.

I know my own story changed when I quit blaming the circumstances of my life on others. I personally required codependence anonymous when I was flailing. When I took ownership and responsibility of me and my life and quit focusing on the behaviors of others, there was a pronounced pivot. There are many spiritual programs and therapists that can provide foundation for change. It is not a flipped switch immediate response but an ongoing growth and continual assessment of ourselves and our place in the world as we peel back the layers and discover more and more about ourselves, our thoughts, feelings and actions.

We have different dimensional states of consciousness. These dimensions available to us on Earth are referred to as 3D, 4D and 5D. These dimensions are not actual places we go but rather they are our individual states of consciousness.

It is likely that a majority of us are moving back and forth between these dimensional states of consciousness depending on where we are in our lives. Perception and perspective are everything.

3D consciousness is viewing things from a purely physical state. You are seen as an individual that is separate from others. Life feels like "the survival of the fittest" and you are identified by the way you look, the job you have, the car you drive and the people you surround yourself with. You feel fearful about missing out or not having enough. Things are perceived as being good or bad and life is a competition. There is not enough for everyone and some people have to miss out. Fulfilment is found in making money and social status. Your thoughts have no power over your reality and what comes your way in life is simply a coincidence. You rely on your five sense to move through the world. We can still experience joy when we are living life from the 3D state but pain and deeper emotions can be difficult to manage. It's a life of skimming the surface with no direction or inspiration to go within and understand any deeper meanings.

4D consciousness begins to awaken to the idea that we are all connected and that there is more to life than what meets the eye. In this state we may understand that our thoughts are powerful and can shift the way reality is perceived. Duality and the idea of good and bad is still experienced, but there is more compassion and understanding behind it. There may be desire for meditation, to leading a more peaceful lifestyle and there is a desire to pay attention to how your actions effect the environment and those around you. In 4D, we may have a strong desire for purpose and to follow our passions. We may understand that life is meant to be enjoyed and that you are worthy to live the life of your dreams. We perceive the world using our 4 senses plus our intuition starts to grow and expand while we seek a deeper meaning to life. We may even experience the synchronistic magic of the Universe.

    Once you reach a 5D state of consciousness, it is very difficult to go back to a 3D state. From this level of consciousness, you begin to understand that we are all one and we are all connected. Life becomes an adventure of growth and there is no such thing as good or bad. There is a higher purpose for all things and every experience holds meaning. You understand that everyone is just on their own journey and everyone is considered to be equal and there is a desire to live from a place of pure authenticity. You understand that your purpose is to live your truth and to seek the joy. From this state, you know that there is no competition and there is enough in the Universe for everyone. You feel overwhelming emotions of love and compassion for life and planet and beyond. Your intuition is clear and you have a deep state of spiritual connection.

    It is important to remember that these states of consciousness are not "better" or "worse" than the other. Every soul on this Earth has their own journey to walk and their own reasons for choosing which dimensional state to live from.

    I truly believe acceptance is the key. If you think about a time when you didn't accept something, how did you feel? Perhaps you got a diagnosis, or there was a break up or a loss of some kind. The longer we resist the reality of truth, the more we suffer. We blame, we rationalize, we minimize, we villainize, we victimize. The unaccepted experience mutates and expands and worsens the way we feel and experience life.

Perhaps feelings of resentment, bitterness or even hate develop.

When we are aware of the reality of our present moment and we accept it as without judgement, fault-finding and criticism, it brings us ease and even contentment.

The hole in our soul could be caused by any past experiences but now, what are we filling it with? It could be alcohol or drugs but it could just as easily be food, gambling, sex, controlling others, judging others, codependency, shopping or whatever. Whatever numbing agents we are using is keeping us from the root cause of our dis-ease or lack of ease. The root cause is the soul sickness and where we must focus. This is where we shift from ego living to spiritual living or 3D to 5D consciousness. As we fill the holes in our soul with spirituality, we start to experience true spiritual healing and health.

If you notice you are often trying to control that which is outside of you i.e. A partner, another's opinion, a pandemic, a habit or whatever, anything that is outside of you, there is variability and therefore always out of control. We can always choose to live in the present moment with access to a power greater than the egoic self. We don't need to wrestle with this notion but just make the choice each day to reconnect to what is required of us. Take inventory, be truthful, be accepting, be grateful and take action and have faith in a connection to a higher power. Inside of you, is where everything matters and where real change can happen.

As I remind myself each day, I will remind you, this is something we practice, not perfect. Keep practicing!

Kelly

To My Auntie, my mentor, and my God-Mother. Thank you for holding my hand on this path of life for as long as I can remember. Thank you for the opportunity to learn and share your story xoxo

"One of the qualities that I admire the most about Bev, is her ability to make anyone, no matter where they are in their life, to feel like the most important person in the world. Even in crowds of hundreds or line ups waiting to speak to her, she is able to focus on the person right in front of her. This makes people feel so valued that they want to continue on the journey of recovery and because of this ability, we will never know how many lives she has saved.

She is one of the most gracious women I have ever met. She is eloquent, loving and kind and has consistently shown me all of the above qualities for over the last 40 years. Her humility shows no bounds." -Kevin D.

"I have known Bev for over 22 years now. I was troubled, living life on life's terms. I had difficulty being a mom, a daughter, an employee and even a friend, despite my desire to change. Bev shared her story with me, how she had changed her life and she gave me hope; something to which I hadn't had for a long time.

I agreed to meet with her weekly and this is when I really got to know her. Not only did she help me change my perception on life, she showed me what it was to be a good friend. Sometimes, I would think I was meeting up for an hour with her and it would turn into 3-hour visits. Not once, did I ever feel I was in her way. As a matter of fact, I felt like I was the only person in the world.

There was even a time when I had a crisis with my eldest son and she cancelled her weekend away to help me through it. I witnessed the most unselfish human I've ever met.

I realized not only was she giving her time and love to me but there were many countless other women she mentored through her lived experience. Her commitment to her program of helping others, mirrored how I could have what she had, if I did, what she did.

Bev never did for me that which I could do for myself but she always helped me get there. Her faith was unlike anything else I'd ever seen. She taught me to pray and to spend time in meditation.

I believed in God but she showed me how to develop a relationship with my higher power through her experience.

I had known Bev for years and not once did she ever talk about her awards or medals. She was so humble. When I asked why she never mentioned that to me she replied it was not important. What was important was the relationships, to do Gods will and the glory was our higher powers, not ours.

When I try to thank her for all she's done for me and my family she reminds me it's our higher power, I need to thank. It's all Gods Grace." – Val W.

"As far back as I can remember, I have known that there is something very, very special about my grandmother. Everyone's face lights up with a smile when she walks into a room.

A few months ago, I attended my first recovery meeting after a friend of mine told me my grandmother was speaking in his town. I showed up and surprised her. I still don't know why I waited until I was 37 to hear her speak, maybe it's because it's the age she was when she decided to get sober.

The church was full and my friend said, "wow, it's busy tonight", to which I replied, "isn't it always like this?" His response, "No, they are all here to see your grandma."

That's my grandmother for you. It was one of the proudest moments of my life. I don't think she will ever truly understand how deeply I feel about her, or just how immense her impact in my life has been. But what we all know is, without a doubt, the world is a better place because of the changes and commitments she made all those years ago. She is one of a kind, and I'm so grateful to call her my grandmother." - Brandon

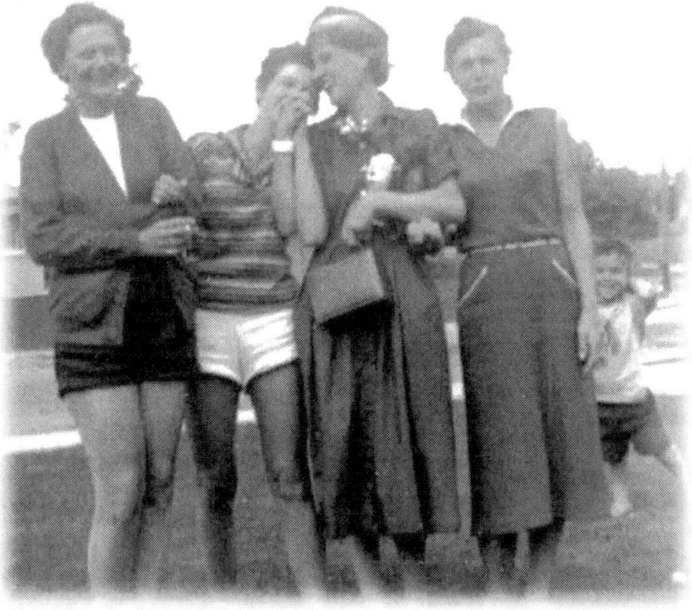

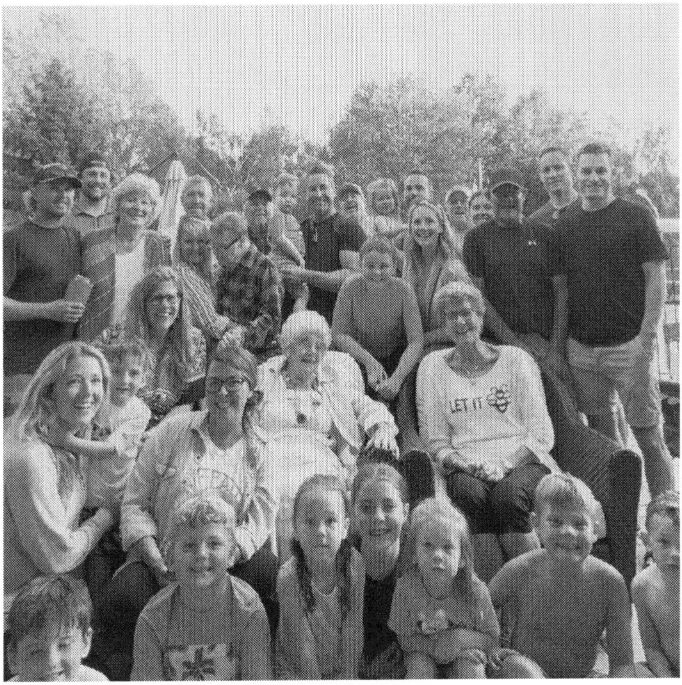
LET IT

Please consider donation to:

Westover Treatment Centre, Thamesville Ontario

https://www.westovertreatmentcentre.ca/

St. Stephens House of London, ON

http://ststephenshouselondon.ca/

Or a recovery centre of your choice

About the Author:
Kelly Spencer is a stress management and mindfulness specialist, empowerment speaker and award-winning author.

kelly@indigolounge.ca

Other book offerings

DESTINY Life & SELF LEADERSHIP

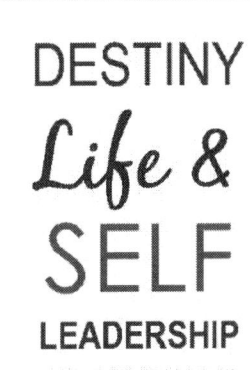

AND YOUR UNLIMITED POSSIBILITIES

Kelly M Spencer

DESTINY Life & SELF LEADERSHIP

28 Day Mindfulness Journal & Dream Manifesto

Kelly M Spencer

grateful.